OUTWARD BOUND
CANOEING HANDBOOK

Third Edition

JOHNNY MOLLOY

FALCON GUIDES

ESSEX, CONNECTICUT

FALCONGUIDES®

An imprint of Globe Pequot, the trade division of The Rowman & Littlefield Publishing Group, Inc.
4501 Forbes Blvd., Ste. 200
Lanham, MD 20706
www.rowman.com

Falcon and FalconGuides are registered trademarks and Make Adventure Your Story is a trademark of The Rowman & Littlefield Publishing Group, Inc.

Distributed by NATIONAL BOOK NETWORK

British Library Cataloguing in Publication Information available

Library of Congress Cataloging-in-Publication Data
Names: Molloy, Johnny, 1961– author.
Title: Outward Bound canoeing / Johnny Molloy.
Description: Third edition. | Essex, Connecticut : FalconGuides, [2023] | Includes index. | Summary: "An illustrated guide to the fundamentals of canoeing, including solid instruction on all aspects of canoeing, from types of canoes to equipment choices, paddle and on-the-water techniques, safety tips, and more. In partnership with outdoor leader Outward Bound, this book combines expert instruction with practical tips to ensure a fun and a satisfying canoe trip for your next outdoor adventure" — Provided by publisher.
Identifiers: LCCN 2022031102 (print) | LCCN 2022031103 (ebook) | ISBN 9781493053087 (paperback) | ISBN 9781493053094 (epub)
Subjects: LCSH: Canoes and canoeing—Handbooks, manuals, etc. | Canoes and canoeing—Safety measures—Handbooks, manuals, etc.
Classification: LCC GV783 .M65 2023 (print) | LCC GV783 (ebook) | DDC 797.122—dc23
LC record available at https://lccn.loc.gov/2022031102
LC ebook record available at https://lccn.loc.gov/2022031103

♾™ The paper used in this publication meets the minimum requirements of American National Standard for Information Sciences—Permanence of Paper for Printed Library Materials, ANSI/NISO Z39.48-1992.

CONTENTS

Dear fellow adventurer:

Whether you're about to embark on your first outdoor experience or your twentieth; whether you're nervous or excited; whether you'll be backpacking, rock climbing, whitewater rafting, or sailing—no matter the recreation type—we believe the outdoors is the best classroom.

That's because we learn best through experience, challenge, adventure, and, most importantly, by being in a community of fellow compassionate people who support us in these efforts. In the outdoors, we find common ground, a place to meet both physically and mentally. We strive together to meet a goal that seems out of reach on our own, but achievable when we work side by side, and through this experience, we see our true selves.

It's this power of community, of taking risks, of being uncomfortable, of saying "no" to mediocrity, of finding refuge from self-imposed limitations that are our real reasons for adventure. These are the reasons why we'll wake up before dawn to canoe with the sunrise, why we'll backtrack 4 miles on tired feet after taking a wrong turn and sing the theme song to *Mission Impossible* to get through it, why we'll fight to stay awake just to stare at the stars in a deep black sky a little longer.

We hope this field guide will lead, motivate, and inspire you to learn new skills and master old ones, to challenge yourself and discover new passions, to strengthen your community, to uncover your deepest strengths, and to remember that it's not about the adventure—it's about every day after.

To serve, to strive, and not to yield.

Josh Brankman
Executive Director, Outward Bound USA

ABOUT OUTWARD BOUND

Outward Bound USA celebrates over 60 years of outdoor education programs that inspire people of all ages to enhance positive change in their own lives and their communities, and to create a more compassionate and resilient world for generations to come. Outward Bound is globally recognized as the leading outdoor experiential education organization, annually serving close to 50,000 youth and adults from across the United States.

At Outward Bound, we believe that principles are best learned when experienced concretely rather than taught abstractly; that when the makeup of a crew crosses racial, economic, or religious lines, differences are celebrated, appreciated, and honored.

Together, we seek, embrace, and value adventure and a life full of learning.

The National Network of Outward Bound Schools in the United States

There are ten regional Outward Bound schools that operate across the United States. Each school has autonomy to deliver Outward Bound courses in their regions and to build strong ties within their local communities and with their regional partners.

Each school develops programs that serve specific student populations or that respond to issues directly affecting their local communities. Here are some examples.

Classic Outward Bound courses take groups of strangers into unfamiliar settings and ask them to tackle challenges *together*. Over time frames ranging from days to weeks to months, students on expeditions gain the social and emotional skills to navigate different types of adversity. While doing this, they move from dependent on their instructors to independent of them, and finally to being interdependent with each other. Throughout that journey, there are many moments that one can often describe only as "magic."

Some schools develop more focused programs that take the classic Outward Bound experience and tailor it for specific outcomes. Intercept has teens and their families work toward common goals and stronger relationships. Grieving Teens provides adolescents with a much needed support group and the skills to work with their grief as they move forward in life from a death loss. Pathfinder aims to ally young adults with their own strengths and helps them to find new purpose in a thriving life ahead.

Every Outward Bound school also works with both educational partners and intact groups of students who, rather than being strangers, know each other. These opportunities tend to be shorter or maybe meet numerous times over a longer period. They have strong outcomes as well and can be just the nudge that some groups need to change their perspective, their teamwork, and their collective mindset.

One specific example of this is the Police Youth Challenge. This course addresses the deeply rooted, fraught relationships between police officers and young people, and endeavors to connect them across issues and identities.

While each school operates autonomously, they all benefit from OBUSA's national network, which ensures a high level of consistency in program quality, safety, and outcomes.

Outward Bound Learning Expeditions

Central to its mission are the values of inclusion and diversity, evidenced by its scholarship program designed to attract and benefit populations that are typically underserved. Nearly 90 percent of Outward Bound participants are eligible for a scholarship or attend free of charge.

In the United States, to advance the mission of "changing lives through challenge and discovery," and to achieve our vision of developing more compassionate individuals and communities, Outward Bound now offers its unique blend of adventure-based programming for a broad range of student populations, including:

- Teens and young adults

- Veterans

- Professionals

- Outdoor educators

- Partnerships with schools and other youth-serving organizations

Outward Bound expeditions are transformative life experiences. With a supportive crew and the outdoors as their teacher, students learn to dig deep to find greater compassion for each other and to push the limits of what they thought they could do. At Outward Bound, teens and adults embark on a journey measured not just in miles of mountain, river, desert, or ocean, but in pivotal character development, leadership skills, and an ethic of service.

Outward Bound Instructors

Outward Bound instructors are highly trained, qualified educators and outdoor skills specialists. Participant safety is a high priority—foundational to every program. Every course is led by instructors who hold, at a minimum, wilderness first responder-level medical certifications, and who have completed many hours of educational, safety, and leadership training.

Instructors are proficient in—and passionate about—the specific wilderness skills of the activity they teach, whether rock climbing, sailing, mountaineering, sea kayaking, canoeing, backpacking, dogsledding, whitewater rafting, or ropes courses. To help students along their personal growth paths, instructors are trained in managing groups and individuals. A vital component of every course is the instructor's ability not only to shepherd students through individual course challenges but also to help them work as effective leaders and contributing members of their team.

Outward Bound's Lasting Impact

The outcomes of each expedition can be noticed while underway. This is true for individuals and the teams they comprise. Social and emotional skills can be observed in action as competence and confidence grow. Becoming a stronger paddler isn't *just* about moving a canoe through the water. It is about awareness, understanding, physical and mental skills, and emotional appreciation of both the activity and the journey. While students may never paddle a river again, some of the perspective they gain will go home with them.

The longer-term impact is different for each student but can be seen in a variety of ways. Many students return home bringing with them an enhanced appreciation for the environment. Others have a new understanding of the commitment and skills required for closer relationships with family and friends. Lastly, there may be a sense of responsibility that leads to improved school performance, or a new dedication to service that they share with friends, family, and their community.

PREFACE: GETTING STARTED

So you want to start canoeing, or want to raise your canoeing skill level and become a competent and complete paddler. Where to get started? Surfing the Web can lead to an avalanche of disjointed information, some no doubt of value, some from unverifiable "experts." In fact, "I read it on the internet" has replaced "I saw it on TV," which replaced "I read it in the newspaper" as a source of information—and misinformation. Those curious about canoeing will be best served with concise, experienced instruction when learning more about this historical and rewarding outdoor endeavor.

That is where this book comes into play. Why should you believe me, Johnny Molloy? I am an outdoor writer with over eighty hiking, camping, paddling, and true outdoor adventure storybooks to my name. I have been paddling canoes for over three decades throughout the United States and Canada and have spent hundreds of nights canoe camping along rivers and lakes and hundreds more on day trips. I have authored and/or coauthored paddling guidebooks for Everglades National Park and the states of Florida, South Carolina, Virginia, West Virginia,

Johnny Molloy

Canoeing can be a shared experience that brings people together. *Stephen Gorman*

Georgia, Tennessee, and Kentucky. I love canoeing and the outdoors and want to share this passion with you so you can join the paddling pastime, make some memories of your own, and perhaps pass on your passion for canoeing and the outdoors to others.

One of your first considerations should be where to canoe. Where you paddle is often a function of where you live. For example, I live in the hills of East Tennessee, where mountain rivers meet valley terrain. The rivers in my area are rocky and pocked with rapids—some with big shoals, some with smaller rapids, all divided by quiet pools. A Florida canoer will ply gentler streams. Someone in eastern Maryland may canoe the tidal creeks and rivers of Chesapeake Bay. A Minnesota paddler will have 10,000 lakes from which to choose. A New Yorker may stroke placid Adirondack tarns. A resident of Washington State may canoe the islands of Vancouver Bay. A Texan from Austin will paddle the crystalline streams of the Hill Country. But no matter where you live (desert excepted), it is likely there are canoeing destinations nearby.

A second consideration is what kind of canoeing do you want to do? Do you see yourself canoeing still lakes or moving rivers? Are you primarily a day paddler, or do you see yourself canoe camping on a gravel bar overlooking a scenic stream or at a backwoods lake? Figuring out where you might feel most comfortable paddling is a smart starting point.

After seeing yourself on the water, seek out like-minded outdoor enthusiasts. If there is one, stop by a local outfitter that sells canoes and paddling supplies. There you can meet other canoers and get a flavor of paddling in your area. Use the internet to find a local canoeing or paddling club, such as those found on Meetup.com. These organizations engage in group trips and always welcome new members regardless of their skill levels. With these groups and clubs you can try different canoes and paddles, see cars outfitted for carrying canoes, and check out the local paddling scene. Also, local clubs organize adventurous paddling trips, helping you explore local paddling destinations. After all, actually getting out there and canoeing is what it's all about.

Your goal is to figure out what types of waters you want to canoe, engage other canoeists, and then explore local canoeing venues. Build your skills with this book and practice to increase your experience; before you know it, waters near and far, large and small, wild and placid, will be your domain. Now get out there and get canoeing!

Canoeing Florida's Peace River on a cool winter day. *Johnny Molloy*

It feels great to be alive and canoeing. *Johnny Molloy*

INTRODUCTION: THE CASE FOR CANOEING

The canoe silently slipped through the translucent water, the calm broken only by drips from an occasionally dipped paddle. A line of tall sycamore trees stretched beyond the morning river fog. Bluffs rose unseen while mussel shell–dotted gravel bars made faint outlines at the river's edge. A slight chill offset the substantial summer humidity. Ahead, a ray of morning light pierced the mist, reflecting off the water, lighting the opposite bank, where a heron silently stalked the shallows. A kingfisher darted across the water, making its frenetic call. Below, shallows revealed crawdads lying motionless, contrasting with minnows darting through the aquatic wonderland. With a silent knowing glance, my brother raised his head and turned back toward me with a smile, acknowledging the sublime scene. It felt great to be alive and canoeing the gorgeous Green River through Kentucky's Mammoth Cave National Park.

When traveling by canoe, whether floating with the current or advancing by the stroke of a paddle, you fluidly move on water through eye-pleasing surroundings, gliding atop waters far flung from our land-based lives. The United States and Canada are blessed with canoeing waters aplenty, from slow-moving blackwater streams drifting into the Atlantic coastal plain, spring-fed waters cutting through rocky canyons, silent ponds lying below towering evergreens, massive lakes with seemingly no shore, and protected coastal areas, where nothing but water, land,

Canoe your way into beautiful scenery such as this. *Stephen Gorman*

and sky extend to the horizon's end. So what's better, a canoe trip to Wisconsin's Sylvania Wilderness, which is primarily stillwater lake paddling, or a float down Florida's St. Marys River, where you let the current do the work? Or would you rather go to British Columbia's Bowron Lakes Provincial Park, to paddle your canoe on lakes and float along with moving waterways? Or perhaps cruise the canyons of Colorado's Green River?

Paddling a variety of waters is just one of the many joys of canoeing. Today's canoer follows the wake of ancestral North Americans who pioneered canoeing in the Northern Hemisphere. (Small, canoe-like boats were independently developed worldwide thousands of years ago.) The name "canoe" is a derivation of the name for dugout boats—*kenu*—of oceangoing peoples first encountered by European explorers in the Caribbean. While dugouts were used elsewhere in continental North America, what is often thought of as an Indian canoe was the birchbark boat used in the Great Lakes area and points north in the massive interconnected network of waterways stretching from Great Slave Lake in Canada's Northwest Territories to the St. Lawrence River reaching the Atlantic Ocean. Of course, farther north still, natives used what today is known as a kayak, but that's another story

Canoes can haul large loads for self-propelled explorers desiring extended adventures. *Johnny Molloy*

Canoes are used by hunters, anglers, bird-watchers, and other nature enthusiasts. *Johnny Molloy*

for another book. When paddling modern-day canoes, we follow the routes of aboriginal Americans, whether it is the mangrove-lined waterways traced by Calusa Indians of the Florida Everglades or the lakes and rivers plied by the Chippewa of Minnesota.

A canoe is a narrow watercraft, tapered on both ends, and propelled by the people floating within its confines. The passengers face the direction of the canoe's travel and use paddles to propel and steer the boat. Today's canoes are generally one- or two-person models. However, many current Outward Bound expeditions use multi-person canoes. Historically, the Canadian voyageurs of the eighteenth century, while engaged in the fur trade, used massive canoes up to 40 feet in length paddled by over a dozen men. Still larger ones were made from massive hollowed-out logs in Central America, the American Northwest, and other places.

Today canoes come in all shapes and sizes, but what has changed the most over time is the material from which they are constructed. The first canoes were wood based, whether dugouts, steam-shaped slats, or birchbark. Hides of animals and, later, canvas were stretched across wood frames. Now canoes are made from high-tech plastics, molded in specific shapes for specific purposes such as whitewater, flatwater, or something in between.

Canoes are renowned for their quiet mode of travel. They silently engage the natural world, with attendant benefits, such as spotting a muskrat determinedly swimming along shore, or an osprey diving into a river, or a smallmouth bass gulping a bug from the water's surface. More visual delights await the canoer, whether it is autumn colors reflecting off an Adirondack lake, a crashing waterfall spilling from an Appalachian tributary, a wood-woven beaver dam on a North Woods waterway, shadows spilling onto a gloomy cypress-lined stream down South, or a sloping gravel bar lying beneath a sandstone promontory overlooking an azure Ozark waterway.

Canoes have a practical side too, especially for the wilderness traveler. Canoes can haul large loads for self-propelled explorers desiring extended adventures. When on a river, travel may simply be a matter of staying in the current, while on a lake, large loads impossible for landlubbers can be transported long distances via paddle power. In other instances ultralight canoes can be portaged between bodies of water, making the connection between lakes, or can be carried around impassable rapids, extending travel possibilities. Canoes need no motor, gas, or oil, and thus don't suffer mechanical breakdowns. They generally don't need a trailer and can be transported by almost any vehicle.

Canoes can take you back to nature's wonders. *Johnny Molloy*

Johnny Molloy

Canoes are used by hunters, anglers, photographers, birders, and other nature enthusiasts. Since paddlers are on the water, it is only natural that canoes are used for fishing, whether on small creeks, fast rivers, or estuarine waterways. Hunters silently stalk ducks and other waterfowl in season. Birders ply aquatic stopovers on migratory flyways to observe winged creatures.

And if you are looking for pulse-pounding excitement, canoers can even tackle whitewater. Situation-specific boats challenge Tennessee's Ocoee River or Maine's upper St. Johns River and a host of other waterways. Milder whitewater awaits boaters on rivers throughout the continent, from Texas's Rio Grande to Indiana's aptly named Whitewater River.

Yet the pleasures of canoeing can be as simple as taking your child on a small lake to spot dragonflies, or exercising in the fresh air, or feeling the sun's warmth overhead. Simply stated, a canoe gets you on the water to enjoy aquatic adventures as diverse as the waterways on which we paddle. Hopefully, this guide will enhance your canoeing experience.

The grace and beauty of a canoe—its curved lines, its elegance on the water when deftly stroked—make a canoe a pleasure to paddle. Take a close look at this self-powered watercraft—it is a boat of many parts.

Look at the top-down view of a canoe, shown here. The bow is the front *area* of the canoe (on the left in photo)—note that it does not refer to a specific part. Just above the tip of the canoe is the bow deck, a small platform that is level with the top of the canoe. Often a handle for carrying the canoe is built into the bow deck. In strictly nautical terms, the left side of the canoe is the port side, and the starboard side is to your right (though this terminology is more often used on larger vessels). The front seat of the canoe is known as the bow seat. This is where the power paddler sits, as opposed to the guide paddler, who sits in the back.

Moving backward, you see the bow thwart, located just behind the bow seat. A thwart is a crossbeam linking the sides of the canoe at the gunwales, the top rails of the canoe. Thwarts support and stabilize the canoe and preserve the canoe's integrity of shape. Only the biggest canoes have a bow thwart.

The largest thwart stretches across the center of the canoe and is centrally located between the front and back of the canoe. It is known as the midship thwart,

A top-down view of a canoe. *David Ramsay*

A side view of a canoe. *David Ramsay*

or, more commonly, the center thwart. Almost all canoes have a center thwart. The last thwart, the stern thwart, is even farther back. Most canoes have a stern thwart. The stern seat sits behind the stern thwart. The rear seat is occupied by the primary canoe steerer. A canoe is one place where backseat driving is encouraged. The unique physics of a canoe means the stern is the most effective position for tweaking the direction of travel. While the stern paddler traditionally turns the boat, the bow person's help is often needed to tilt, turn, or rotate quickly or to stop or back paddle. The rear person plays a particularly important role in any kind of current. The stern deck is behind the stern seat. It too is a small platform, often with a built-in carrying handle. The stern is the back of the boat and, like the bow, is an area rather than a specific part of the canoe.

Now examine the side view of a canoe shown in the accompanying photo. The gunwales (also spelled gunnels) are the upper rails of the canoe. The gunwales run atop each side of the canoe from tip to tip, bow to stern. The bow deck and stern decks are connected by the gunwales. The waterline is the point where the surface water meets the canoe. Draft is the depth of boat under the waterline. Freeboard is the distance of the canoe from the waterline to the top of the boat. The length of the canoe is measured from tip to tip at its longest. Waterline length is the length of the canoe at the surface of the water. The thwarts and seats are connected to the canoe by nuts-and-bolts hardware.

So what does all this mean, and how can it help you become a better canoer? Knowing the parts of a canoe and canoe terminology will familiarize you with the aspects and functions of a canoe. You will then understand how the parts work together and what you can do to tailor a canoe to suit your paddling needs.

So with that in mind, let's delve a little deeper into canoe parts. Canoe seats, and by that I mean the original seat that is built into the boat—as opposed to an aftermarket product that you add to the already existing canoe seat—come in a variety of materials. Traditional canoe seats are framed in wood, usually ash, with pressed or woven cane in the center where you actually sit. Cane is aesthetically pleasing, easily drains water from a wet paddler, and dries quickly, but it is less durable. Another choice is nylon webbing woven into the wooden seat frame. Nylon webbing doesn't dry as quickly as cane but certainly lasts longer and is my choice. Some canoes come with molded plastic seats. I don't recommend them. They are hard, hot in the summer, and cold in the winter, and they also don't drain water from a wet paddler, though some have built-in drain holes. On the plus side, some molded seats include backrests and cup holders. Aluminum canoes have aluminum seats with many of the same characteristics as the molded plastic seat.

Nylon webbing doesn't dry as quickly as cane but certainly lasts longer. *Stephen Gorman*

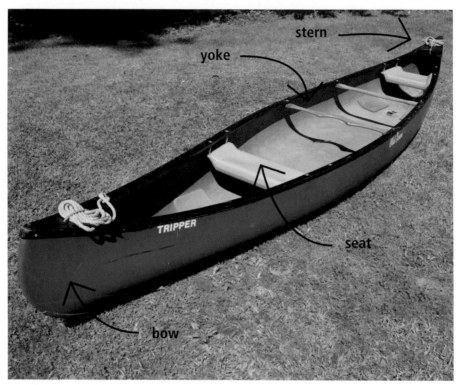

A tandem canoe. *Stephen Gorman*

A tandem canoe, of course, has two seats, situated in the front and the back as described above. A solo canoe is normally shorter than a tandem, with a seat in the middle. Whitewater paddlers sometimes use what is known as a saddle. In that instance, paddlers straddle a low seat that is connected to the canoe on the bottom, not the sides, and place their knees on the bottom of the boat with their feet pointed back. This gives them a lower center of gravity and also increased stability when bracing their legs around the saddle. A middle seat can be added to tandem canoes. Plastic snap-in seats simply fit over the gunwales. Obviously, this is for mild waters.

Most canoes have only two thwarts. Thwarts are mostly made of wood, though there are plastic- and metal-thwarted models—metal for ultralight canoes and plastic in cheaper boats. Wooden thwarts have a "reverse hourglass" shape—the ends are narrower then widen in the middle. The middle is wider (and sometimes thicker) to bear pressure from the canoe body continually twisting in varying waters and from the loads within the boat. The curved thwarts add aesthetically alluring lines too. The center thwart, or midship thwart, is the largest of the thwarts. It

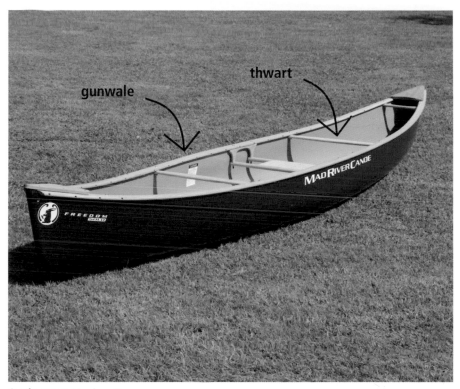

A solo canoe. *Stephen Gorman*

also has the curved "neck ring" for portaging your boat, even if it is only from the garage to the car. Aftermarket portage yokes, with padded shoulders, can be attached to the center thwart.

Gunwales can be plastic, metal, or wood. Plastic gunwales rarely fit snugly and often have gaps between the gunwale and the canoe itself. Metal gunwales retain their integrity but can get warm, and metal residue will sometimes rub off on a paddle if the paddle regularly contacts the gunwale. Wood gunwales are the most expensive and the most aesthetically appealing, but they are also the heaviest and need a little upkeep, as well as being prone to warping and problematic in extreme climates.

Canoes from various manufacturers come in a dizzying array of configurations. Learning the parts of a canoe will help you understand what you are looking for.

Canoes and the places to paddle them are as varied as the people in the canoes. When looking for a canoe, consider what kind of paddling you'll be doing as well as potential destinations. Will you be canoeing through still bodies of water or moving rivers? Will you be cruising big lakes or perhaps the ocean? Or negotiating mild shoals? Or drifting down sluggish streams? Will you be going down rivers with significant stretches of whitewater, where you may take bone-jarring hits from rocks? Your answer, like my answer, may be a little bit of everything. We want to paddle everywhere!

When choosing a canoe, contemplate material and design. The most widely used canoes come in a wide array of oil-based materials and are molded for weight, performance, and durability. A few wooden and some aluminum canoes are still built today. Don't waste your time or money on an aluminum canoe. Although known for durability, you shouldn't buy one unless you expect it to endure extremely frequent use by inexperienced paddlers, such as at a summer camp or a canoe rental outfitter. Aluminum canoes are extremely noisy, which detracts from

Canoes come in a wide array of oil-based materials and are molded for weight, performance, and durability. *Stephen Gorman*

the outdoor experience, and the metal surface is more likely to get hung up on underwater obstacles rather than slide over them. They are hot when the weather is hot and cold when it is cold.

Most wooden canoes are handmade. These beauties are often displayed as showpieces and are infrequently paddled by their builders. Other old-time natural-material canoes include birchbark, cedar, and canvas. Fiberglass was once favored as a canoe-building material but proved heavy, brittle, and not durable.

Since most canoers rule out wood, aluminum, and fiberglass, oil-based materials such as ABS, polyethylene, Kevlar, and even graphite are favored. In the molding process the plastics are often layered, with each layer providing qualities such as resilience, buoyancy, and/or strength while keeping the weight down as low as possible. It is this relationship between quality and weight of materials that often determines the price of a canoe. For example, a high-end canoe will be both durable and light, while a mid-range boat may be somewhat sturdy and moderately heavy. A still cheaper canoe may be very heavy and not durable at all.

Specialty canoes are constructed to handle specific situations, such as ultralight portage-friendly canoes for Minnesota's North Woods, or a whitewater boat designed to dance through tricky rapids. Though we may wish for a flotilla of specialty canoes, most of us end up with one boat. I prefer durable, multipurpose canoes and thus seek out the tougher composites such as TuffStuff, where basalt fibers are woven with oil-based fibers to create canoes that can be dropped off buildings and survive!

Canoe design is composed of the following factors: length, width, depth, keel, rocker, bottom curve, flare, and tumblehome.

Length: Length of a typical canoe can range anywhere from 9 feet for a single-person boat that is easy to lift on and off a car to 20-foot behemoths used for extended wilderness expeditions. Your average two-paddler canoe ranges from 14.5 to 17 feet in length.

Width: Wider canoes are more stable and can carry heavier loads but are slower. They can also be less responsive and slower turning. Narrow boats track better but are tippier. A wider boat with more stability would be ideal for a family with young children, whereas a canoe racer will seek a slender boat for slicing quickly through the water.

Depth: Depth is the area from the top of the gunwales to the bottom of the canoe. Deeper canoes can carry more weight and shed water but can be heavy and open to winds. Shallow canoes are sleeker but can take on water over the gunwales in rapids or big lake waves. Again, go for the middle ground.

Keel: Keel is a nautical term for the centerpiece underlying a boat from bow to stern, to which the frame of a boat is attached. For canoes, the keel is the ridge running along the bottom of a canoe from front end to back end. The farther a keel extends from the boat's bottom, the better the boat tracks in open water. However, a pronounced keel inhibits a paddler's ability to turn the boat quickly. A keel helps for tracking in lakes, but decreases maneuverability in moving water. Flatwater canoes may have a pronounced keel, while whitewater canoes have virtually no keel. Nowadays very few canoes have an actual keel protruding from the boat, save for aluminum canoes, where the keel marks the weld between the sides of the boat.

Rocker: This is the curve of the keel line between bow and stern. More rocker increases maneuverability at the expense of stability and speed. Flatwater canoes will have minimal rocker, therefore less boat in the water, which means less resistance.

Heavy Rocker

Moderate Rocker

Straight Line

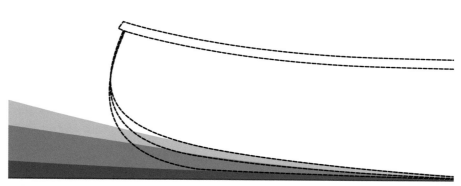

Rocker. *canoeing.com*

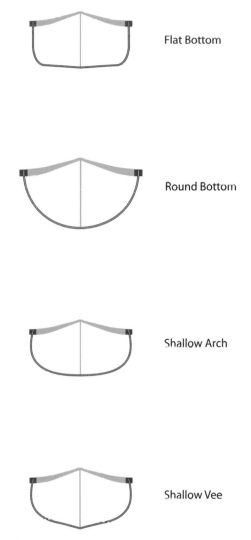

Flat Bottom

Round Bottom

Shallow Arch

Shallow Vee

Bottom shapes. *canoeing.com*

Bottom curve: This is how it looks—the curve of the canoe bottom from one side of the boat to the other. The more curved the canoe bottom, the less stable the boat, and it isn't as fast crossing flatwater, simply because a deeper bottom curve means more water friction and the paddler has to push more boat through the water. On the other hand, whitewater boats have a more curved bottom for quick responsiveness in whitewater. A shallowly arched boat is more efficient than a flat-bottom boat, but not as tippy as a deeply curved boat.

Flare: Flare is the outward curve of the sides of the boat. This outward curve sheds water from the craft and pushes water away from the boat. How much flare you want depends upon how much whitewater you expect to encounter. Flatwater boats have little flare, because more flare means more friction between the canoe and the water.

Round Bottom

Flare. *canoeing.com*

Tumblehome: Tumblehome is the inward slope of the upper side of the canoe, from the middle of the canoe sides up to the gunwales. A more inwardly curved tumblehome allows paddlers to get their paddle into the water easier but also decreases available space inside the canoe. Whitewater boats, which require more skilled, swift, and precise strokes while in rapids, have more tumblehome, allowing easy paddle access to the water.

Situation-specific canoes, such as whitewater, racing, or portaging canoes, use all the above design features for maximum efficiency. Whitewater boats have heavy rocker and deeper flare for maneuverability, but are a zigzagging tub on lakes. Portaging canoes are built with extremely light materials, but ultralightweight portaging boats can sacrifice durability. Multipurpose boats tweak the features to become a paddler's jack-of-all-trades. So what boat is best for you?

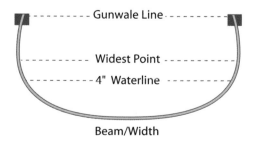

Tumblehome. *canoeing.com*

Multipurpose boats are a paddler's jack-of-all-trades. *Keri Anne Molloy*

Most of us can't afford a separate canoe for flatwater paddling, solo paddling, whitewater paddling, fishing small streams, and portaging between big lakes. If you are going to have one boat, I recommend a multipurpose touring tandem canoe, one with adequate maneuverability so you will be able to adjust and react while shooting rapids or make quick turns when floating toward a submerged log while taking a picture, yet still be able to keep a straight line on a lake. Consider a boat that can navigate moderate whitewater, handle loads expected on an overnight canoe camping trip, and track decently through flatwater so you can sightsee along a lake shoreline instead of constantly steering the boat.

But why a tandem versus a one-person canoe? A solo paddler can use a tandem canoe simply by weighting the front to make it run true. A larger canoe also allows a solo paddler to adjust positions according to conditions. However, you can't change a solo boat into a two-person boat without difficulty. Two-person models allow someone else to share the special moments experienced while silently sightseeing on a lake at sunset or running a rapid on your local river. So unless you are a dedicated soloist, go for a two-person canoe.

The primary canoe I use is the Old Town Penobscot 164, long a favorite of mine. It is a great all-around boat that I have used on varied trips, from day paddles on local East Tennessee rivers to 100-plus-mile Gulf of Mexico treks to Maine waterways to surprisingly small streams, over years and years. At 16 feet, 4 inches in length and weighing 58 pounds, it is not too heavy for one person to load and unload from the car. It works for me.

But each individual canoer should select a canoe to fit his or her specific purpose. I also have an ultralightweight canoe for North Country adventures. Designed to be carried from lake to lake via portages and paddled in between, I highly recommend the 17-foot Wenonah Spirit II. At 42 pounds this ultralight Kevlar boat can perform in the water and not break your back on a portage, so you can get between lakes more efficiently, minimizing your time on land.

I suggest getting a canoe with muted colors that blend into the land and water, integrating with nature rather than standing apart from it. However, colorful boats can be had, from candy-apple red to yield-sign yellow. Bright colors can be helpful if a canoe needs to be spotted by rescuers—something to consider in the far north or remote, hazardous areas. All else being equal I prefer a green boat. I can hide it in the brush or woods if necessary, and while on the water nature's beasts and other paddlers won't get eye shock.

Other Considerations When Choosing a Canoe

ROOMINESS

The larger the canoe, the greater freedom of movement. You can not only move your head and shoulders around but also shift your whole body to stretch your legs, or extend your arms for bird-watching or for better casting while fishing.

ENTRY AND EXIT

When choosing a canoe, imagine yourself getting in and out of the boat in a variety of settings—from a dock or a beach, along a wooded shore, while in shallow water, or while partly submerged in a rapid. Smaller, narrower, less stable boats will require more dexterous canoeists, whereas a wider, larger, more stable boat makes for easier entry and exit.

A CANOE IS THE MOST OPEN OF BOATS

A canoe is literally open to water coming in, whether from an accidental tipping or rain. When getting in and out of a canoe, water will often gather at the bottom of the boat, dripping off your feet. This can be troublesome or irritating. More dangerous, however, is when the canoe begins filling with water while going down

Perpendicular entry. *Stephen Gorman*

a rapid, which brings the gunwales closer to the water, allowing still more water to accumulate in the boat until it becomes entirely filled with water, spilling the paddlers and their belongings. Ponder the various design features of a canoe while weighing the possibilities of water getting in your canoe. For example, a widely flared boat sheds water.

SPEED OF TRAVEL

How fast do you want to travel? Are you interested in covering lots of water? Or do you want to use your canoe as a nature observatory or fishing platform? Or do you see yourself amiably plodding on a lake near the family cabin? The type of material and design of boat will affect its speed. An aluminum canoe, for example, has more drag versus the sleeker skin of an oil-based boat. Consider water resistance in canoe design. The more a boat is created for quick maneuvering (which usually means a wider boat), the more water resistance it has. Conversely, racing boats (more often narrow) are designed with minimal resistance. Lower-profile canoes have less wind resistance and thus are easier to paddle while traveling against the wind. Any gear or part of a person rising above the gunwales is subject to wind resistance.

HOW MUCH STUFF DO YOU WANT TO CARRY?

Since you can load so much stuff into a canoe, you often do. These big loads can be not only weighty but also cumbersome and bulky. Many times I have seen paddlers piling their canoes so high with gear that the rear paddler could hardly see the front paddler. Other times the gunwales were barely above the water surface, unable to handle more than the tiniest of waves. Be careful arranging your loads. Too much stuff can and will get in the way of your overall outdoor canoeing experience. When looking for a canoe, visualize the boat with the amount of gear you expect to take along.

Conclusion

Everyone knows their own style, desires, and budget when choosing a canoe. Running through the preceding checklist of factors will help you determine the canoe that works for you.

Canoers need more than just a canoe to embark on an adventure. Your accouterments will help get you down the river, across the lake, and over to Grandma's dock in safety and comfort—depending on which canoeing necessities and accessories you bring along.

Paddles

A canoe isn't much good without a paddle. You've heard the saying, "up a creek without a paddle." A paddle is the means by which a canoe is moved and is the connection between you and the water. Finding the right paddle may mean the difference between a good day and a not-so-good day on the water (there are very few bad days when canoeing!). Wood is still popular as a paddle material (and is my preference), though plastics dominate the market, especially in lower-end paddles such as those used by canoe liveries, and also in ultralight, high-end paddles. Some cheap varieties combine a plastic blade with an aluminum handle. Lately, more canoers are using double-bladed paddles favored by kayakers, though most double-bladed canoeists are solo paddlers.

A wooden canoe paddle. *Stephen Gorman*

The bent-shaft paddle blade is offset at an angle, allowing the blade a better "dig" into the water.
Stephen Gorman

When examining a canoe paddle, start at the top and work your way down. The top of the paddle is the grip. The two basic grip forms are a T shape and a pear shape. The T grip is shaped like the letter T and is easiest to grasp and keep in your hand, which makes it popular with whitewater paddlers. The T grip is also better for novice canoers and children, since the top of the paddle doesn't slip from their hands while in mid-stroke. The pear grip is more ergonomic, sort of rounded at the top, which allows the paddle to move effortlessly in your hand stroke after stroke after stroke. That is why the pear grip is preferred by flatwater canoers.

Canoe shafts connect the grip to the blade. The shafts may be rounded or oval. When paddling, you grip the shaft with your lower hand while your upper hand holds the grip atop the paddle. Some argue that oval-shaped shafts are more ergonomic than rounded shafts. Bent-shaft paddles—literally bent at an angle between the grip and the blade—are popular among flatwater canoeists in both bow and stern.

On a bent-shaft paddle, the paddle blade is offset at an angle from the paddle shaft, allowing the blade a better "dig" into the water. The angle puts the blade in a more powerful position, adding an advantage that can be helpful over long distances. Bent-shaft paddles are efficient when trying to get from point A to point B, but offer less control when it comes to precision steering moves.

How about a square versus rounded blade? I prefer a rounded blade for precision strokes, whereas a power paddler, likely the bow paddler, will desire a square blade to strike more water surface with each stroke. Rounded blades drain water from the paddle more quickly than do square blades, making each stroke a little easier. A complaint against square blades is that they can catch the water surface when the paddler reaches forward to make the next stroke. Whitewater paddlers sometime prefer square-bladed paddles in order to get more blade into shallower water.

There are other blade shapes in flatwater paddles: beavertail and ottertail, to name a couple. They are deeper, narrower blades that work especially well in deeper water and when you want a faster cadence.

Paddles can vary in length as well, generally ranging from 48 to 60 inches (or longer). All things being equal, a longer paddle will provide more power; a shorter paddle, more quickness. Paddler height, boat, seat position, grip preference, and paddling needs should also be considered.

I recommend a shorter paddle for the stern paddler, because that is the person who makes continuous small adjustments in boat direction while traveling. A shorter paddle is easier to maneuver when making all these small adjustments, not only in the water but also when shifting the paddle from one side of the canoe to the other, largely because you don't have to raise it as high to get it out of the water between strokes.

Factor in paddle length with the canoe you plan to use. A wider canoe will require a longer paddle.

Finding the paddle length that works for you is also relative to your height. A taller person will want a longer paddle. Longer paddles can become unwieldy, while shorter paddles are easier to handle, but each offers unique benefits.

Paddle blade width and length is another concern. Wider paddle blades displace more water, allowing the canoer to move the boat forward faster, but the more water displaced, the more effort it takes to move the paddle through the water. Some paddlers prefer smaller blades, thinking that executing easier, more efficient, but more frequent strokes is ultimately better than fewer but more draining strokes.

Arctic aboriginal peoples originally used a long, thin blade but sat low in kayaks. The long, thin blade allowed the paddler to access more area from that position. In contrast, a canoer sits more upright and thus digs deeper—at more of a downward angle—into the water, so getting the blade to the water is less of a concern. The most popular blade size is 20 by 8 inches. Specialty paddle blades can be curved or cupped. These single-purpose blades are ultimately for speed and

Finding the right paddle for you may mean the difference between a good day and a not-so-good day on the water. *David Ramsay*

You may make literally thousands of strokes during a canoe trip. *Johnny Molloy*

don't serve the multiple demands the typical canoer will place on a paddle. Cupped blades are preferred by whitewater paddlers to maximize the grab on the water, but they do not work well backward.

Some canoeists use double-bladed paddles, which have a blade on both ends of the shaft, resulting in more efficient stroking. They are most popular with smaller one-person canoes and with kayakers, but a typical canoe is too wide for a double-bladed paddle to realize the efficiency gained when using one with a narrow kayak. Almost all double-bladed paddles are two-piece, snapping together in the middle. This makes them easier to haul around and it allows paddlers to offset the blades for more efficient stroking. Double-bladed paddles average between 7 and 8 feet in length.

Think about paddle flexibility. Some woods bend more than others; for example, spruce paddle shafts are stiff, while basswood shafts are more flexible. Whitewater canoeists want a stiff, responsive paddle for fast, decisive strokes, while flatwater canoeists want something with a little more give to ease the burden of repetitive strokes. Composites exhibit an array of flexibilities depending on the type of material used in the paddle.

You may make literally thousands of paddle strokes during a canoe trip. Paddle weight becomes a factor with each successive stroke. The lightest paddles are expensive composites, carbon fiber, and the like. Consider if you really want an expensive paddle that is going to take abuse from rocks, sand, banging around in a car, being borrowed by your clumsy cousin, and so on. Weight-wise, the lightest paddles come in at 14 ounces or less, while average paddles are 30 to 40 ounces. Ultimately, it is an immensely personal choice, and paddlers should embrace the uniqueness of every individual's paddle needs and preferences. No matter what paddle you choose, consider personalizing it. Paddles can be modified/decorated with paint, varnish, stickers, tape, or cord to identify it as your paddle among others and to reflect your passion for canoeing.

Carrying an extra paddle while canoeing is a wise idea, especially when whitewater canoeing. Paddles break or can get lost in a tump. It's easy to stow an extra paddle in your canoe—simply put it out of the way at the bottom of the canoe, or tie it lengthwise along the inside of the boat between a thwart and canoe seat. The latter method keeps the paddle out of the way but with your boat in case you capsize. The disadvantage is that if you need your spare in a hurry, such as in a rapid after losing the paddle in your hand, then getting your spare paddle unknotted and free may be troublesome. If paddling a loaded boat, store the extra paddle between gear bags or boxes where it doesn't move around yet is quickly accessible.

Life Vest

There's a reason life vests were invented. Accidents can happen while canoeing. A paddler wearing a life vest will be markedly better off when unpredictable troubles arise than a canoer not wearing one. Think of life vests as seat belts on the water. I always have a life vest with me, and it's the law just about everywhere these days. I carry a high-quality life vest, not only for safety but also for comfort. The better kinds allow for the freedom of arm movement that is essential for canoers. Consider spending the extra money on a quality ergonomic life vest, both for safety and for the ability to paddle while having your vest on. Try different models on at the store and feign paddling (with or without a paddle).

Commonly known as PFDs (personal flotation devices) these days, life vests come in a wide array of styles and fits, with specific models for men, women, anglers, kids, and even dogs! Most quality vests have multiple points of adjustment to fit the PFD around a canoer's waist, shoulders, chest, neck, and arms. More points of adjustment make the vest more comfortable whether you are wearing a

T-shirt in the summer or multiple layers in colder conditions. Additional features on a PFD include reflective trim, a tethered emergency whistle, use-specific pockets (for knives, sunscreen, lip balm, etc.), and nonessentials such as color.

Angler PFDs are not only designed for freedom of arm movement, but they also come with an array of pockets to store line, flies, pliers, and more. Some even have a drop-down mini-platform to use for tying on lures. Boat hunters use camouflage models. Women's PFDs factor in bust size; some models even adjust for varied chest sizes and have built-in support. Further choices include longer- or shorter-waisted PFDs, and yes, there is a little more attention to style. Others use neoprene that molds to fit unique body shapes over time.

Inflatable vests are small and very light, making them ideal for canoeing in hot climates. They are strapped on uninflated, but when troubles arise, or when trouble is anticipated, you simply pull a cord and the PFD instantly inflates, powered by a replaceable air canister. Inflatable PFDs also have an oral inflation mode in case the canister fails. Manual inflation–only vests are less popular but still available, sometimes used by flatwater paddlers who very infrequently encounter situations in which they would need their PFD.

Accidents can happen while canoeing. *David Ramsay*

A child's PFD. *Stephen Gorman*

Dog PFDs come in a wide variety of sizes to fit Fido whether he weighs 10 pounds or 120 pounds. Of course, dogs don't care for them much, no matter how comfortable, but if safety is a priority for your pooch, then spend the money for one.

Even more so than for dogs, PFD fit is of paramount importance for a child, as an ill-fitting vest can be disastrous in a water emergency. Children's life vests are sized for kids of all ages and sizes. Some PFDs have reinforced shoulders to withstand tension when pulling a child from the water. Infant life vests are also available. The comfort as well as safety of an infant is important, since an uncomfortable baby will let you know by crying.

Good PFDs aren't cheap, so it pays to take care of them. Dry them after each use, to prevent mildew from growing on them. After drying, store them in a cool, dry place to prevent rot from heat and sun. They are best stored hung from a rack off the ground. If your vest becomes soiled or moldy, scrub it in a solution of soap and water. A small amount of bleach mixed with water may be needed to rid your vest of mildew. Clean out and open the pockets too. If you have been in salt water, rinse your vest off with fresh water. Since PFDs are often only used seasonally then stored for months, they can last for many years but will deteriorate over time. Make sure and replace your vest if it's too old—after all, it may one day be a lifesaver.

Chair Backs

After a long day in a canoe, infrequent paddlers sometimes start reaching behind themselves, rubbing their lower back, which is sore from sitting on an unsupported canoe seat. The best defense against back pain is training to build core strength, develop technique, and learn proper body positioning. If and when pain strikes mid-paddle, switching positions (between sitting and kneeling on both knees or with one knee down) can bring relief. But even hardened paddlers are prone to "canoer's back" on multiday trips. Attachable backs for canoe seats offer support that can keep you comfortable over long paddles. If the manufacturer of your canoe sells chair backs, choose its brand first, because they are designed to fit on your boat.

However, many aftermarket canoe chair back models exist. These add-on chair backs hook on to the canoe seat to provide support for your back. Look for one with lumbar support. Chair backs range from bare plastic skeleton supports to cushioned models that rival your easy chair at home. Unfortunately, finding the best one to fit your specific boat is a real hit-or-miss proposition. Beware of elaborate metal and canvas chair backs with connecting straps that can get in the

Chair backs for canoe seats ease the burden of a long day in the boat. *Johnny Molloy*

way of paddling. Be prepared to purchase a chair back, bring it home, and fit it on your canoe. Get in the boat and try paddling. Imagine being in there for hours, paddling and moving around. I have seen many chair backs get used once and then cast aside because they didn't attach properly, slid around while paddling, got in the way of paddling, inhibited an angler's casting, or interfered with birders using binoculars. Ask around, borrow a chair back, and be prepared to return a purchased one. However, finding a chair back that works for your canoe is worth the effort.

Dry Bags

Waterproof dry bags are one of those inventions that give modern canoers an advantage of leaps and bounds over those of yesteryear. Gone are the "bad old days" (not that long ago) of storing your gear in plastic garbage bags or plastic buckets. Plastic bags have plenty of advantages—they are cheap, easy to pack and compress, and can be used as internal liners. With the ubiquity of quality dry bags, though, single-use plastic is falling out of fashion. Dry bags, primarily made of rubber and/or plastic, have various means of closing themselves down that result in a watertight seal, keeping your gear dry as you travel waters oceanic or riverine. Most closure systems involve rolling the open end down, then clipping the rolled end tight to keep it closed. Dry bags can range from tiny, personal-size, clear dry bags in which you might throw things such as sunscreen, keys, bug dope, and a small box of lures, to massive rubber "black holes" with built-in shoulder straps and waist belts designed not only to keep your stuff dry but also to use for canoe portages. Of course, in our information age, there are specialty rubber bags and plastic waterproof cases into which we can fit our smartphone. Many of these also have a lanyard that goes around your neck to prevent your phone from getting lost. Some phone bags even have floats on them.

Dry bags come in all sizes and shapes, many designed to fit in the tiny corners of an open canoe. They can be long and narrow to hold a tent, or wide to fit most anything. When non-portage canoe camping, I use several separate dry bags, dividing what I store in them by categories. For example, I keep one clear personal-size dry bag close by with sunscreen, camera, bug dope, and lip balm. I'll use another dry bag for clothes and sleeping bag, another for camping gear such as tents and camp chairs, and still another for cooking equipment and non-cooler food. Dividing gear according to type saves you from frustrating searches to find what you need. When in portaging canoe country I consolidate, generally using the biggest dry bags with shoulder straps for comfortable load carrying on

Dry bags come in all sizes and shapes, many designed to fit in the tiny corners of an open canoe.
Keri Anne Molloy

portages and compromising with multiple types of gear in one bag. Some people use smaller dry bags inside a portage pack. This protects the dry bags as all abrasion is taken by the pack and not the dry bags inside. Fewer bags are more efficient to carry. Furthermore, the fewer individual items you are portaging, the fewer you will forget.

Speaking of multiple dry bags, consider dividing important items such as lighters, extra reading glasses, medicines, and so on in two separate dry bags while on long canoe trips. If disaster strikes, such as a bag-losing spill into rapids (which has happened to me) or accidentally leaving a dry bag at a portage, you won't be out of luck.

Do not skimp on quality when purchasing dry bags. Cheaper bags are thinner and will puncture or rip more easily. Soaked sleeping bags, soggy food, or lost keys can be disastrous on a canoe trip. Spend the extra bucks to get the good stuff. One final note: Clip or tie down your dry bags to your boat when you are canoeing in rough water; that way your dry bags (and gear!) will stay with the boat if you take a spill.

An assortment of dry bags. *David Ramsay*

Ropes

Competent paddlers will have ropes, also known as painters, fastened securely onto each end of their boat. These ropes can initially be used to tie the canoe onto the vehicle en route to the canoe venue. During the trip the canoer can use them to tie on at a dock or shoreline log while loading or stopping. For whitewater canoeing, painters should not be tied. You want them to come free if needed. They should be attached via bungees or pushed underneath bow and stern float bags.

Competent paddlers will have ropes, also known as painters, tied onto each end of their boat. *Stephen Gorman*

You can also rope your boat through shallows or rapids. Painters around 8 to 12 feet long and no bigger around than your thumb should be sufficient for the job. When not in use, tie the ropes to the canoe seat thwarts. Yet another way is shown in the photo.

Plastic Boxes

Plastic storage boxes, found at any mega-retailer, come in a variety of sizes and shapes and are ideal for canoe camping trips. They are inexpensive, easily fit in the bottom of the canoe, and can double as a table at camp. Store items in here that you don't want smashed, such as bread. However, they are not nearly as waterproof as a dry bag. Consider using these if you are on flatwater or gentle rivers and are not portaging.

Portage Yokes

Portage yokes are padded shoulder pads that you can mount to the thwart of a canoe to make portaging more comfortable. This aftermarket item aids greatly not only in comfort while portaging but also balance while carrying the canoe. Again, go with the canoe manufacturer if it provides an aftermarket yoke for your brand and model canoe.

Knee Pads

Knee pads for canoeing are not worn around your leg as in sports, but are glued to the bottom of the canoe for comfort when you paddle with your knees down on the canoe bottom, rather than with your feet on the bottom of the boat. This paddling position is taken when more power is needed, or when you need a lower center of gravity while canoeing through rough water. Knee pads provide cushion, especially desirable while bouncing through whitewater, and establishing a more secure connection with the canoe.

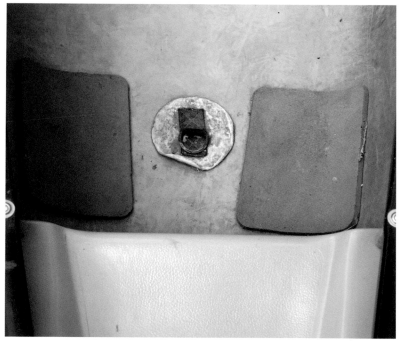

Knee pads. *Stephen Gorman*

Foot Braces

Foot braces also add power to paddle strokes. A foot brace is usually a metal rod or wood plank glued or screwed to the canoe, against which paddlers places their feet to transfer power to the stroke rather than to the legs. They can also be made of plastic or foam and are sometimes adjustable.

Splash Cover

A splash cover is a waterproof cover fitted over the canoe with snaps. They are used to prevent rapids and waves from splashing over the gunwales into the canoe. Complete covers have openings for the paddlers only—the rest of the boat is covered. Other splash covers will only shield each end of the canoe. Splash covers are used primarily by canoers tackling heavy whitewater or big lakes in the North Country.

A splash cover prevents water from spilling over the gunwales into the canoe. *Stephen Gorman*

Anchor

Lightweight canoe anchors are good for river trips where no portaging is required. They come in handy if you want to fish moving water without the boat moving. However, they do weigh the boat down. In portaging country there is no need to carry a full-fledged anchor. Modern anchors, weighing mere ounces, are made of plastic straps that resemble a bucket, which can be tied to a rope and then to the boat. Simply find a big rock, set it inside the plastic mesh, and an anchor is born. But be careful when anchoring. Once, on the Chattahoochee River in Georgia, my

29

Though you will want the proper canoeing accessories, your experience on the water is what it's all about. *Johnny Molloy*

friend anchored his canoe below Buford Dam. We were having success fishing, and neither the warning sirens of an impending dam water release nor my strongly worded suggestions could persuade him to pull up anchor. The water release came and soon engulfed the canoe, tipping us over and sending us downstream. We lost everything, including the canoe, the fishing tackle, and my wallet. The lesson? Think before dropping anchor.

HOW FAR DO I GO
AND OTHER TRIP PLANNING CONCERNS

When contemplating how far to travel during a canoe trip, take into account the many other time-consuming activities other than just paddling—loading the boat and gear at home, stopping along the way for last-minute items, setting up shuttles if river tripping, unloading the boat from the car, loading the boat on the water, and more. Make sure to leave time for floating and relaxing. To this end, I try to keep my daily paddling mileages reasonable. If I had a dime for all the "our trip took longer than we thought" stories I've heard, I could buy a new canoe. In other words, paddlers often want to make the most of their trip and cram in more distance than is feasible.

How far you go depends on what type of waters you canoe. For example, if canoeing a river, you will be aided by the current, which varies from stream to stream and even within that one river, depending on the particular stretch of river. If lake paddling, wind can be a factor, whether it blows with you or against you, or both. If paddling coastal zones, you should factor in tides, which may work in your favor or against you, or both.

Consider day trips on moving streams first. Obviously trip lengths depend on mileages between put-in and take-out. You want to give yourself ample time to

How far you go depends on what type of waters you canoe. *Johnny Molloy*

cover the water. Winds can be a factor on streams, too, but not to the same degree as on open lakes and bays. Factoring about 1.5 to 2 miles per hour is a good starting point. This allows stopping time, lunchtime, and let-the-river-take-us time. Next, consider your other pursuits. Will you be fishing? Swimming? Bird-watching? Do you want to explore gravel bars? Take pictures? Look for wildflowers in the riverside woods? Permit ample time for non-paddling pursuits. Allow for plenty of daylight to finish your float, remembering that hours of daylight depend on time of year. Also, give yourself time to drive the post-paddle shuttle. It is always easier to load your boat and return to your starting point while daylight reigns.

When day paddling on a lake, you will most likely be starting and ending at your point of origination, saving shuttle time and hassle. Otherwise, the pre- and post-paddle chores and times needed to do them are the same as river canoeing. However, since lake paddlers won't have a current in their favor, travel time must be factored differently. I suggest starting with an estimate of 1 to 1.5 miles per hour travel time, though stronger paddlers may work with 1.5 to 2 miles per hour. Wind speed and direction will certainly affect your progress. If you are paddling with the

When paddling on a lake, you likely will be starting and ending at your point of origination, saving shuttle time and hassle. *Johnny Molloy*

Coastal paddlers need to factor tides into their arrival and departure times. *Johnny Molloy*

wind, it can literally be a breeze getting from point A to point B. But the return trip may be as challenging as the initial paddle was easy.

Time of day when canoeing on a lake can greatly alter your trip. Winds are generally lower in the morning and evening, kicking up when the sun heats up the day, and are generally strongest in midafternoon. Winds bring waves every time. Fronts and thunderstorms will alter this general pattern.

One advantage lake canoeing has over river canoeing is not being locked into a certain distance that has to be covered. When river canoeing, you set up shuttles and then must commit to going all the way to your exit point where the shuttle vehicle awaits. Lake canoers, on the other hand, can simply shorten or lengthen their trip as conditions and desires warrant. As on a river paddle, be sure to factor your non-paddling pursuits into your lake paddle when you plan your trip.

Coastal paddlers absolutely need to factor in the tides—both high and low tides. Tidal currents will affect your speed, and at slack tide there is no current. Timing your trip with the tides can be tricky. Where you are relative to the coast will affect the exact time and strength of the tide. Paddling against a tidal current can be exhausting. Also remember that outgoing low tides will leave some areas high and dry that were covered with water a few hours earlier. In open, coastal areas winds will be a factor. The same rules apply for winds and time of day in coastal zones as they do on lakes. When trip planning, work from a starting point of 1 to 1.5 miles per hour and then lower your estimated travel times if paddling against the tide or pursuing other activities. Be very conservative with time estimates in coastal estuarine areas. Adversity can arise—the tide turning against you, shallow water, winds kicking up, having to work around dry tidal flats, and negotiating heavy winds and waves.

Canoe Trip Planning: A Cautionary Tale

A canoeing friend in northern Wisconsin was eager to guide me down the Badger State's St. Croix River, a National Wild and Scenic waterway that flows through the Great North Woods before heading south and forming the boundary between Wisconsin and Minnesota.

My Wisconsin friend, Ellie, asked me to pick a section of river I wanted to float, and she would accommodate the request, as she had already paddled most of the river. I picked a 60-mile segment, from Gordon Dam to Sand Rock Cliffs. This segment offered fine fishing for bass, pike, and panfish, as well as scenic camping at designated riverside sites.

Ellie and I took off, casually floating and fishing, letting the river push us downstream. That night around the campfire, I mentioned our nearly ideal river progress, averaging 15 miles per day on this fast river. This pace would lead us to our desired endpoint in a four-day trip.

That was when Ellie mentioned this was a three-day trip—she had to be back at work the day after the third day. I had assumed we were out for four days. A simple misunderstanding of dates suddenly turned what was initially a casual canoe camping trip into a paddle-athon. We pushed hard those last two days, marking mileage, stroking the paddle hour after hour. It was painful to pass through so much scenic river so fast.

Don't let this happen to you. Before you start a paddle adventure—whether it is canoe camping or day tripping—get together with fellow members of your party to review your trip plan. Go over the practicalities of the event including who, what, where, when, and how far. You also need to discuss gear, especially gear to be shared by the group, whether boats, cooking items, tents, even who will drive.

When organizing a group canoe trip, consider the following issues: group size, group dynamics, and trip expectations. The more people in a party, the more complicated things become. For canoe campers I suggest keeping your group small, as this offers the best outdoor experience.

I prefer to keep canoe camping groups no bigger than four somewhat like-minded people. Too many people and personalities require too much smoothing over of different

Review your trip plans before starting any canoeing adventure. *Johnny Molloy*

expectations before and during your canoe trip. You may not want to mix your hard-partying old college roommate with the deacon at church.

Trip expectations are very important. Everyone needs to be on the same wavelength as to what the trip will be like. For example, is everyone willing to paddle 12 miles in a day or will someone want to stop earlier? Does everyone want to paddle hard all day long and spend minimal time at the campsites? Or do they want to spend more time telling canoe tales by the fire than actually canoeing? Make sure everyone is in agreement about the length and style of canoe trip.

Also, make it clear up front about sharing expenses, chores, and other duties so there will be no unpleasant surprises when it comes time to collect money—or wood. Even after all parties have come to an agreement about the adventure, review the details one last time. That way you won't end up paddling all day down a river—like I did—because of a simple misunderstanding.

I did a lot of dumb things during my college days at the University of Tennessee while learning about life in general, as well as learning about the canoeing life. Knowing river levels before launching my canoe was an important lesson.

Winter had clearly lost its grip. The warm spring sun begged a canoe outing. My friend John Harv Sampley and I headed for the nearby Emory River. At the put-in we were greeted by surging, brown waters boiling just below the treetops of riverside trees. My college buddy and I launched anyway. At first we were enthralled by the exceedingly high waterway. Then we dumped on a curve, the first of several such occasions. What were normally rocky shoals had morphed into brawling swells that simply swamped the canoe with huge waves. Harv and I couldn't appreciate the spring scenery as anticipated—we were too busy trying to keep the boat upright and saving our lives! Ironically, the previous summer we had come to the same put-in, and the river was so low we couldn't even float past the first rapid.

On both occasions we were too ignorant and inexperienced to check water levels before we left. Knowing water levels is crucial for paddling a river. High water levels can mean muddy and dangerous waters, which often obscure hazards such as logs and boulders. Muddy water is a higher possibility in spring and summer. Low waters can result in getting stuck in shallows, dragging your boat, or simply not being able to proceed downriver unless you are willing to carry your canoe!

Nowadays, checking river levels is simply a matter of getting online. The Water Resources Division of the US Geological Survey measures water flow rates on most rivers in the United States at frequent intervals. The US Army Corps of Engineers, various power companies, and assorted other government entities collect similar information. Flows are recorded in cubic feet per second (cfs) and/or gauge heights, and are available to everyone.

The key variable is the height of the river at a fixed point. Gauge houses, situated on most rivers, consist of a well at the river's edge with a float attached to a recording clock. The gauge reads in hundredths of feet. Rating tables are constructed for each gauge to get a cfs reading for each level. All this information is useful for planning river trips.

Gauge information also can be obtained quickly online, often along with recent rainfall. Make use of this information and compare it using paddling guidebooks or local outfitters that recommend minimum, ideal, and maximum flow rates of a given river. Not only do the gauges give you the current river levels, but they also detail the historical flow data for the time period in which you intend to visit. River level averages vary throughout the year. Generally speaking, river flow rates

Paddler on a placid stretch of river. *Keri Anne Molloy*

average highest in late winter and spring, then make a slow decline through the summer into fall. Snowmelt, storms, and hurricanes can turn average flow rates on their head. Always check water levels on the section of river you plan to float *before* launching.

Knowing water levels helps you know what size rapids to expect. *Johnny Molloy*

Rivers and streams run cooler in the spring. Lower spring air temperatures combined with cold water make accidents and hypothermia a real possibility. And canoers, just like Harv and I, eager to get on the water after winter, will sometimes venture out despite cool temperatures and higher water.

Runnable rates for all streams and rivers have not been established. Runnable rates are based on having enough water to float down the river but not so much flow paddlers will be in peril. When considering runnable rates, factor in your skill level, the type of boat, and the weather. However, if you frequently float a favorite river, you can record the flow rates and river levels each time you canoe the river. Establish your own flow rates and water levels at which canoeing is best for you. These self-determined best flow rates can differ depending on canoeing activities— you may want slower, calmer water for fishing and high, fast water for running rapids.

USGS real-time water data for the United States can be found on the internet at http://waterdata.usgs.gov/nwis/rt. This in-depth website has thousands of gauges for the entire country, updated continually, and graphs showing recent flow trends along with historical trends for any given day of the year, available at the touch of your finger.

Establish your own flow rates and water levels at which canoeing is best. *Keri Anne Molloy*

Canoers should keep apprised of lake levels too. A variance in lake level will not make or break your trip such as river levels can, but lake levels can affect your paddle. For example, Fontana Lake borders Great Smoky Mountains National Park in North Carolina. Canoeists often ply Fontana Lake to access Smokies campsites and trails bordering the lake. In late fall the impoundment is drawn down in preparation for coming winter rains and snowmelt. When Fontana Lake is drawn down, the exposed mud lake bottom makes accessing Smokies campsites and trails a potentially messy nightmare. Canoers land on slick, muddy slopes, slopping their shoes and perhaps their gear en route to the shore. At full pool, Fontana Lake canoers can land on, well, land. Canoers knowing lake levels can time their trips accordingly.

Finding lake levels takes a little research. If a lake is impounded, then levels for that lake can most often be found on Army Corps of Engineers websites or regional water management district sites. After finding the current lake level, make sure to also find the full pool level, to use as a measuring stick. Dammed lakes are best enjoyed at full pool. Natural lakes often have gauges as well. In Minnesota, gauge information is collected by the Minnesota Department of Natural Resources. These natural lakes follow much the same pattern as rivers do: high in spring and

Canoers knowing lake levels can time their trips accordingly, such as here on Fontana Lake. *Johnny Molloy*

lowering through the summer. In Montana, some lake levels are monitored by the US Bureau of Reclamation.

Knowing tides is key for coastal canoers. Paddling in estuarine waters is on the rise, from Washington to Maine. Unlike rivers, tide flows switch directions periodically. A poorly timed paddle can leave you fighting the tidal current to and from your destination, or having no water to paddle at all! Local tide information can be garnered from GPS units, weather radio broadcasts in coastal areas, and a host of private and public websites.

Tides can be your enemy or your friend. Low tides can leave you stranded in mudflats, or they can effortlessly pull you where you want to go. Tides can be a directional indicator as well. If you know the general times of tidal variation in a given area, you can tell which way is the ocean and vice versa. I once spent the night lost in Everglades National Park, near the Roberts River. The next morning I knew the tide was outgoing and checked it, then followed a series of creeks out to the Roberts River toward the Gulf of Mexico, thus regaining my position. Knowing the tides can be a great help in numerous areas. Try to time your travel with the tides!

Canoer looking over low tide. *Johnny Molloy*

Savvy canoeists will do a little research before hitting the water, whether they are on rivers, lakes, or the salty sea. A little knowledge can prevent unpleasant surprises and allow greater opportunity to maximize your precious time on the water.

As with any outdoor adventure, canoeing has its hazards (although I believe that simply driving and day-to-day living in a big city is far more dangerous than your typical canoe trip). The following are some potential canoeing hazards and how to handle them. Remember that your mind is your most valuable tool, and panic is your worst enemy. Always take a moment to consider the situation and your options of how to deal with a hazard before acting.

Rapids and Shoals

Rapids and shoals are fast-moving sections of a stream or river. They are usually shallow spots where the river drops, often located at the confluence with a tributary stream. Canoers should generally aim for passages between rocks, sandbars, logs, and other obstacles in rapids. Rapids are categorized using a difficulty rating system that classifies conditions from Class I to VI. Class I has easy waves requiring little

Canoers going through a rapid. *Stephen Gorman*

maneuvering and few obstructions. Class II rapids may have more obstructions and require more maneuvering, and the rapids may be flowing faster. Most recreational canoers paddle waterways within the Class I to II range, with occasional Class III. Class III rapids can be difficult, with numerous waves and no clearly defined passage, and require precise maneuvering. Class IV to VI increase in difficulty, with Class VI being unrunnable except by experts.

Be prepared for the rapids on your chosen waterway before you embark on a trip. Know the paddling skill level of your *entire* party and match their abilities with the appropriate river or section of river. Once on the water, if you are not sure about the route through a rapid or its difficulty, pull over and scout the rapid—the whole rapid, from top to bottom. Don't go in blind. (I did this once in Minnesota's Kawishwi River and tore a hole in a rental canoe, ruining our trip and costing us hefty repair bills.)

In simple rapids or shoals, look for a tongue of water forming a V shape, the wide part of the V facing upstream from your downstream point of view on the rapid. Aim your canoe toward the middle of the tongue—the point of the V—and flow through the rapid at the rate of speed that the current takes you. Under most circumstances, do not speed up when approaching a rapid—this is akin to hitting the gas when driving through a busy traffic intersection. The bow paddler should be

In simple rapids or shoals, look for a tongue of water forming a V shape, the wide part of the V facing upstream. *Stephen Gorman*

ready to tweak the front of the canoe away from obstacles, either by punching the obstacle with the paddle or simply stroking toward the chosen passage and away from the obstacle. The bow paddler also must look for underwater obstructions that are perhaps not visible to the stern paddler. If an obstacle is seen, the bow paddler, for example, calls out to the stern paddler, "Rock 20 feet ahead on the right."

One of the thrills of whitewater canoeing is that both paddlers play important roles, with both taking responsibility for turning and moving the boat forward, backward, or side to side. The stern paddler is perhaps *more* responsible for steering, but the bow paddler can see obstacles sooner and respond quicker, often indicating to the stern paddler what she needs to do.

Again, steer the canoe into the rapid, but don't gun it. Avoid excessive slaloming around obstacles. Fast turns in faster water can be more difficult to accomplish than they look and require split-second decision-making. Try to plan a route completely through the rapid when possible. Smart paddlers will pull over to the shore and scout rapids. Some rapids, though, are simply too long to assess from beginning to end. On a long rapid you must read the immediate water in front of you while scouting ahead for upcoming obstacles and passages. Be methodical and don't panic. Ride the rapid, don't rush it. And remember, you aren't through it until you are *entirely* through it.

Scouting a rapid from shore. *David Ramsay*

If you become stuck in shallows or rocks, do your best to keep the direction of the boat parallel to the flow of the water. A canoe turned sideways to the flow will rapidly fill with water then be driven into a rock, wrapped around said rock, and ruined. If you are stuck, take a moment to quickly plan your escape, including where you want to go once freed—don't just pop off the obstacle willy-nilly. The paddler closest to the obstacle should attempt to push off the obstacle with a paddle to dislodge the canoe. If that doesn't work and no other options are available, hop out on the *upstream* side of the boat and dislodge the canoe. Do not step out on the downstream side, as that may lighten the canoe and set it free, knocking you over or causing a leg injury, especially if a foot gets stuck in rocks. Safety first! Again, take care to keep the boat parallel to the flow when dislodging the canoe.

If your canoe does turn sideways and fill with water or begin to tip, lean downstream. This is very important. Leaning into an obstacle is better than leaning away from it. Eventually this may mean climbing out of the canoe onto a big rock, for example, but this is better than an injury or a canoe flipping upstream and becoming seriously pinned. The power of current pushing into a canoe is stronger than two paddlers can handle. A filled canoe can become inextricably lodged against

A filled canoe can become inextricably lodged against a rock, break in half, or go where you don't want it to. *Johnny Molloy*

Proper technique for floating a rapid if capsized. *David Ramsay*

a rock, break in half, or go where you don't want it to. If tipping downstream, try to get out, shift the partly submerged boat parallel to the flow, then dump or bail the excess water. If you do flip your canoe and the boat is facing upstream and filling with water, try to turn the partly submerged boat upside down, then flip it back up with the open side facing downstream. This can be very difficult.

Most important, keep your cool if stuck in a rapid. Panicked canoers can turn minor mishaps into major ones. If you do fall into the water, lie on your back with your feet facing downstream at water level. Dangling feet can get stuck in rocks, then trap you underwater. And don't lose your paddle! You will need it later, after you recover.

Whitewater canoeing can be hazardous, but is also challenging, diverse, and highly rewarding. If you want to explore whitewater, it is a good idea to take a class on appropriate preparation, reading the river, paddle strokes, and tactics and rescues.

Strainers and Sweepers

Strainers are fallen trees, limbs, or logs lying in moving water. They can lie singly or in piles left over from high-water events. Strainers can be very dangerous for canoers. You may be casually floating down a stream, unaware that a freshly fallen tree is atop the water. If you do nothing, your canoe will hit the strainer and dump you over, perhaps becoming lodged in or under the tree, pinning you as well. Avoid strainers by keeping watch downstream and vigorously paddling away if you see one ahead. You may have to pull over to the shore and carry your boat around a stream-wide strainer. Sweepers are fallen trees or branches in and above the water that will "sweep" you into the water as your canoe flows into them.

Winds

On all waters, but more so on lakes and open waterways, wind can be the paddler's worst enemy, though a moderate tailwind can be a good thing. So can an insect-clearing breeze. But big blows can be dangerous. Whether storm driven or typically strong spring afternoon gusts, big winds do occur. Heed small-craft advisories when issued by the National Weather Service. Wind forecasts can be obtained from a weather radio or the internet and can be vital to your trip. Listen to the forecasts carefully—they predict wind speed and direction too. Try to plan your trip around the wind; when this is unavoidable, consider canoeing smaller bodies of water and using the lee sides of shores and islands to minimize the effect of the wind. Avoid being pushed into a shore where waves are crashing. If you get too close to shore, turn your canoe into the wind and waves, paddle directly away from shore, then readjust your route to head where you originally planned to go.

Waves

When the wind blows, the waves come right along with it. First-time canoers at places like Everglades National Park, Lake Superior, Yellowstone Lake, and other open-water destinations are often shocked at the size of waves they encounter. A powerful wind can blow a glassy bay into a choppy wave trap. Wind may slow your progress, but waves can capsize your craft—real trouble. Make sure any valuable loose gear is tied tightly to the boat. When big winds are expected, try to paddle early in the morning when the winds and subsequent waves are generally lower. Consider paddling in the late afternoon or at night (using a GPS downloaded with topo maps or nautical charts) for the same reason. As a rule I try to start early, not only to avoid the winds but also to give myself ample daylight to handle any unforeseen circumstances.

In big waves, try to modify your route to stay in sheltered waters, or at least take breaks in sheltered waters when you can, to avoid exhausting yourself. Don't

Canoeists have to be careful in waves and wind, especially in open water. *Johnny Molloy*

try to fight through waves. Roll over them, ride the crest, and drop into the trough as gently as possible, then pull yourself up and over the crest again—"Ride 'em; don't fight 'em."

Canoeists have to be careful in waves and wind. First, try to avoid getting parallel to big waves, as they can go over the gunwales and swamp your boat. If you are heading in a parallel direction, paddle through them at an angle, zigzagging back and forth, not directly parallel to the waves. A wave crashing into the side of your canoe can be a quick capsizer. If water is splashing in, try to bail at intervals; otherwise the water coming in will lower the canoe, allowing more water in faster, finally culminating in a sinking. Have a bailing cup ready before entering big waves. Beware waves coming from behind; they can drop a lot of water in your boat when you are not looking.

When leaving the beach or other open shore in big water, aim your canoe straight toward the waves. Try to time your departure between wave surges, then paddle into the waves. Do not allow your boat to get broadside to the waves—it will get filled with water and pounded back to shore.

Tides

Tides can be friend or foe, much like the wind. If you time your travel with the tides, the paddling can be carefree. Low tides can leave you stranded in mudflats and shallows. Tides may merely cause discomfort or delay, but they can do real damage in other situations. Be careful around man-made canals; a strong pull can take you where you don't want to go or ram you into a tree lying half-submerged in the water. The biggest problem with tides comes when cutting corners in rivers, peninsulas, and straits. You may be paddling in one direction, but the tide is flowing perpendicular to your direction, catching the nose of your canoe and turning you over before you know what happened. Watch for signs of direction flow in the water ahead of you, such as ripples and currents, then adjust your speed and direction.

Powerboaters

On bigger lakes and rivers, canoers will encounter motorized boats. Powerboaters are much like the winds and tides: They can either help you or hinder you, depending on the speed and direction they are going. Many waterways are multiple use, and it's important that canoers and powerboaters share these waters responsibly.

On bigger lakes and rivers, canoers will encounter motorized boats. *Stephen Gorman*

49

Powerboaters are not the enemy. It is not us versus them. Powerboaters can aid in giving directions and help in an emergency. But they can also speed by without consideration. It all depends on the driver. Be a defensive paddler, watch and listen for motorboats, then exercise the same courtesy toward powerboaters as you would expect from them.

7

CANOEING SAFETY

Preparation is the best plan for safe canoeing. Before leaving home, go through your canoeing checklist (See Appendix A in the back of this book for a canoeing checklist). Check water levels and weather conditions, then get out there and enjoy your special time on the water. The following are additional guidelines that will help you stay safe and focus on enjoying the beauty of a gliding canoe over scenic waters.

Wear Your Life Vest

This is canoe safety rule #1: Wear your life vest. Canoeing accidents and deaths are rare, but most involve drowning, and the victim is almost never wearing a life vest. Bring your life vest along and wear it. This is the single easiest thing you can do to make your outing a safe one. These days, whether they are simple vests or whitewater rescue PFDs, there is no reason not to have a comfortable vest with the features you want. Each paddler must have a life vest in the boat, so play it smart and wear yours.

Always wear your life vest. *Johnny Molloy*

Canoe Entry/Exit

Canoe entry/exit is another area of potential mishap. Paddlers often enter or exit the canoe with wet feet, which sometimes causes slipping. Factor in wet feet and a wet canoe bottom when getting in or out of the boat. Additionally, the canoe may not be stable when paddlers enter/exit the boat. As the paddler gets in or out of the canoe, the boat moves with them, which can result in a spill. Before entering or exiting a canoe, make sure the boat is stabilized, either securely grounded on land or tied onto a dock.

To enter the canoe, usually the bow paddler holds the canoe while the stern paddler enters the boat first and becomes safely seated. Next, the stern paddler plants their paddle in the ground or holds onto the dock while the bow paddler enters the canoe. Make sure all parties are ready to embark before leaving the shore or dock.

To execute a safe exit with two paddlers landing ashore, the stern paddler again stabilizes the boat by staying seated and planting the paddle into solid ground. The bow paddler exits to shore then holds the canoe stable from the shore while

The stern paddler plants the paddle into solid ground, stabilizing the canoe, then the bow paddler exits. *Johnny Molloy*

the stern paddler exits. If landing at a dock, each paddler should first tie an end of the canoe to the cleats or pilings, then the stern paddler holds onto the dock, stabilizing the boat, while the bow paddler exits. The bow paddler then holds the boat from the dock while the stern paddler exits the canoe.

Nonslip sandals or water shoes help with slipping issues when entering/exiting. Be positive the boat is stabilized before entry/exit, then move slowly and deliberately, making sure the other canoer is aware of your intentions to enter or exit. Once while on Florida's Yellow River, a friend and I landed the canoe on a sandbar. My buddy hopped out of the front of the boat. I stood up in the rear, absently surveying the surroundings. He then proceeded to jerk the canoe farther ashore. When he pulled, I fell backward from my standing position in the canoe smack into shallow water! Always keep your partner in mind while getting in and out of the canoe—and moving it.

Lightning

The summer day started bright but clouded over as the afternoon heat wore on. My brother and I were canoeing in Arkansas's Buffalo River. I could hear thunder

Lightning can strike a canoer—and with fatal results. © *Yegor Piaskovsky/Dreamstime.com*

somewhere in the distant Ozarks. What could we do but get our rain jackets out and scout for safe harbor? The storm hit and the rain came in torrents, followed shortly by sharp crackles of lightning and wind so strong it was snapping limbs from trees. We paddled frantically and finally came upon a high vertical bank with a gravel bar below it. My brother and I hastily landed, then stood with our backs to the high bank, shuddering with every crackle and flash of each lightning bolt. Lightning can strike a canoer, and with fatal results. Think about it: You are floating on water with a canoe paddle pointed skyward. Be wise and make a plan beforehand. When you see or sense a storm coming, know what you will do when it hits. Get off the water immediately; if you can't land at that moment, paddle directly along the shoreline, preferably beneath overhanging trees. After leaving the canoe, seek shelter in a low area or in a grove of trees—not against a single tree—then wait it out.

Sun

When canoeing, the sun can be your enemy and your friend. You welcome it in the morning as it lights the world and warms the day. Once you are on the water and in your canoe, the sun tries to burn your skin, penetrate your eyes, and kick up

Be prepared for the sun from head to toe. *Keri Anne Molloy*

Always remember sunglasses and sunscreen. *Johnny Molloy*

gusty winds. Finally you lament its departure every night as darkness falls. Sun can be a real threat no matter where you are. But canoers feel the power of old Sol even more because of the reflection of the sun on the water.

Be prepared for the sun from head to toe. Use sunscreen and wear a wide-brimmed hat, a bandanna for your neck, and long pants and a long-sleeve shirt. Clothes are your best defense. Put on sunscreen before you get out in the sun. Cover your hands and feet. I have personally seen several cases of sun poisoning on canoers' hands—pale-skinned neophytes who figured their hands wouldn't be affected. If you think about it, however, while canoeing your hands and arms are outstretched and soaking up the sun, even if they are moving much of the time.

Sunglasses can be not only protection for the eyes but also an important tool for the canoeist. Regular paddlers should invest in sunglasses that provide 100 percent UV protection and are polarized. Polarized glasses eliminate the reflective glare off the water surface and allow you to see into the aqua below, which will help you navigate shallows and enjoy the often fascinating aquatic habitat underwater. By all means bring a neck strap for your sunglasses. Not only can you take your sunglasses off and not have to worry about losing them or dropping them in the water, but they will always be handy around your neck. On extended canoe trips, consider bringing some premoistened lens cleaner wipes so you can see your best while keeping your eyes protected.

Heat

Heat is normally associated with the sun. Heat problems are likely to occur when canoeing still waters on really hot, windless days. Prevent heatstroke before it happens. Follow the tips above to protect yourself from the sun. While paddling, take shade breaks and swim to cool off in the heat of summer. I once floated the length of the Grand Canyon in midsummer and cooled off by repeatedly swimming with long pants and shirt on. Try to travel in the cool of the morning or evening if possible.

Cold

As an outdoor writer and spender of much time in the wilds, people often ask me, "When is the coldest you have ever been?" My surprising answer: "Canoeing in the spring." In our eagerness to hit the water, especially after a string of nice March days, canoeists take off for the nearest river, disregarding the facts that

Play it ultraconservative in cold water. *Stephen Gorman*

twenty-one days of March are classified as winter, and lakes and rivers can be really cold then (or not even iced out up north). A windy day of canoeing with air temperatures in the 50s and water temperatures below that will numb wet feet and wet bodies. If you tump, or tip over, the possibility of hypothermia is very real here. Play it ultraconservative in cold water. Always have dry clothes with you, stored in a waterproof dry bag. Seasoned cold-weather paddlers often resort to dry suits, wet suits, and neoprene socks and gloves to counter a cold-weather tumping. Remember, if you wear rubber boots to keep your feet dry, those same boots can become a water-filled burden if you tump your canoe and end up swimming for the shore. Again, always wear your PFD. It will also keep you warm in cold conditions.

Try to keep your feet dry entering and exiting the canoe, and sponge out the boat as necessary to keep water in the canoe from wetting your feet. Thunderstorms can turn a hot day into a cold one before you know it. A rainsuit can be invaluable—lightweight ones pack easily in a canoe. Prepared paddlers should have one along at all times. It is easier to stay dry and warm, or even just dry and not so warm, than to get wet and cold then try to warm up.

Snakes

Canoers often see snakes in freshwater areas, especially rivers. Some snakes prefer being near the water, and you should watch out for them, especially on sunny streamside rocks, which is a preferred area for copperheads in some regions of the United States. I have seen other snakes swimming atop the water while I floated by in a canoe. One snake, while crossing a big lake, was so tired of swimming it tried to get in my canoe! If you leave a snake alone, it will generally do the same for you.

Canoers will see snakes in freshwater areas, especially rivers. *Johnny Molloy*

Bugs

Sometimes when canoeing we consider the possibility of death by blood loss from mosquitoes, but actually your chances of dying from a bug bite while canoeing are less than your chances of dying on the car ride to the canoeing venue. Watch out for ticks, which may carry Lyme disease, and spiders. Check for ticks after spending time in the woods, after every canoe trip, and at least once a day on multiday trips. Bee stings are a real danger to those who are allergic to them. You know who you are, so make sure you have some Benadryl and epinephrine in the canoe.

Medical Kit

Medical kits have come a long way. Now you can find activity-specific medical kits that not only pertain to your chosen activity but also come in different sizes for each activity. You can find a specific kit for everything from backpacking to adventure racing. Medical kits designed for water sports such as canoeing come in waterproof pouches. I recommend Adventure Medical Kits (www.adventuremedicalkits.com). The company carries a good variety of kits and also divides its kits into group-size units. So whether you are a solo canoer or on a multiple-boat, multiple-day river trip, you will have not only the right kit but also the right size one.

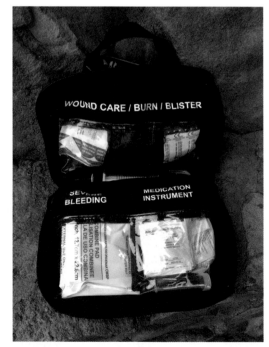

Group first aid medical kit. *Johnny Molloy*

8

THE STROKES

I was fortunate enough to be introduced to canoeing at a young age. Over the course of several years and a lot of trial and error I learned how to paddle. I observed other canoers, learning what to do and what not to do. But mostly I learned by being in a canoe on the water. After you have been doing it for some time, paddling is similar to driving a car with a stick shift—it becomes second nature. However, learning this way has its disadvantages, mainly that you may end up with bad canoeing habits. But for the most part, the canoe strokes that are taught in canoeing courses are the same ones paddlers use when self-teaching, simply because these are the strokes that work.

I believe there are three different strokes that will help you through most situations, based on my thousands of miles of paddling in diverse waters. My advice is to keep it simple. Learn the basics, then advance to more complicated strokes. If you are a novice canoer, the best place to learn how to paddle and steer the canoe is in flatwater, such as a pond or lake, where you don't have to contend with current.

When canoeing, the "aim" is to guide and advance the canoe, making it go where you want it to. Every paddle stroke, no matter whether done in the bow or

Flatwater—ponds or lakes—is the best place for novice canoers to learn how to paddle and steer a canoe. *Johnny Molloy*

stern, tends to turn the canoe. And from that tendency is born the *J-stroke*, which is named for the movement of the paddle as you end the stroke. A J-stroke moves the boat forward but keeps it tracking where you want to go, rather than moving haphazardly forward.

First, grasp the top of the paddle, the grip, with one hand and place your other hand midway down the paddle shaft. Reach forward and immerse the paddle blade into the water. Keep your torso upright. Next, pull the paddle parallel with the boat, moving the canoe forward, with the paddle blade perpendicular to the direction you are traveling. The J part of the J-stroke comes as the paddle moves behind you.

When you reach the end of the stroke, curve the blade of the paddle outward, away from the canoe, ending with the paddle blade parallel to the direction of travel. This outward curve of the paddle blade away from the boat keeps the boat straight. No matter whether you are paddling on the left side of the canoe or the right side, make your J-stroke outward and away from the boat. The amount of curve in your J should be the amount needed to keep the canoe straight, no more. A competent stern paddler will do the boat guiding, leaving the bow paddler to mostly execute straightforward power strokes, with less J in each stroke.

Start of the J-stroke. *Stephen Gorman*

Finishing the J-stroke. *Stephen Gorman*

The *draw stroke* also moves the boat forward and keeps it straight. It's almost the opposite of the J-stroke, in the sense that you are pulling the boat and the paddle together rather than having the paddle and canoe go apart at the end of the stroke.

With one hand on the paddle grip and the other hand a little below midway on the shaft, reach out and forward from the canoe, this time leaning outward a bit versus keeping your torso straight as with the J-stroke. Plant the paddle blade into the water at an angle away from you.

Next, begin to draw the paddle toward you and the canoe. At first the boat will move slightly toward the paddle. You then follow through—this is what makes the boat move forward—with the paddle stroke running roughly parallel to the canoe. Again, the bow paddler will be executing more straightforward power strokes rather than steering the boat.

Using the draw stroke and the J-stroke, paddlers can keep the canoe moving forward, yet simultaneously steer it to keep the boat going where they want it to go. Over time you will develop an infinite number of small stroke variations that will guide the canoe exactly where you want to go while simultaneously factoring in wind, current, and tides. Be patient; you will become an accomplished paddler over time. Remember, the longer your paddling day, the more efficient you want to be with each stroke.

Finishing the draw stroke. *Stephen Gorman*

The third stroke is the *sweep stroke*. The sweep stroke is used to turn a canoe around, primarily in flatwater. For example, if you had paddled into the lake from a lakeside cottage and wanted to turn around and return to the cottage dock, you'd use the sweep stroke. Much like the name implies, the canoer sweeps the paddle outward from the boat to turn.

Grasp the top of the paddle at the grip with one hand and position the other hand about 40 percent down the paddle shaft. Next, stretch the paddle outward, nearly parallel to the water. Dip the lower half of the blade into the water and make a nearly 180-degree stroke, ending with your paddle blade parallel to the boat. It may take several of these to completely turn the boat around. The other paddler should be sweeping as well to turn the boat in an arc.

Note: Stern paddlers are relegated to guiding the boat simply because that is where the boat is best steered. The bow paddler can tweak the direction of the canoe, but is mostly absolved of steering detail. No matter the waters, the stern paddler always gets more steering duty. Consider that before you claim your position in the canoe.

Whether you are in the stern or the bow, cooperation between paddlers is necessary for efficient and graceful movement of the canoe. Generally speaking, the bow paddler strokes on whichever side of the canoe works best for the paddler, and the stern paddler, who can look forward and see the movements of the bow

Cooperation between paddlers is necessary for efficient and graceful movement of the canoe. *Stephen Gorman*

paddler, adjusts to the side that the bow paddler is using, usually paddling on the opposite side of the canoe from the bow paddler.

On a long paddling day, consider your body position, core strength, and technique. Switching positions—from sitting, to kneeling on both knees, to one

The stern paddler reacts to which side of the canoe the bow paddler is using. *David Ramsay*

knee down—can make a big difference and bring relief from one position to the next. Proper technique can help relieve lower back pain and other pain from potential overuse. Paddling is much easier to sustain with a strong core. Regular core strength exercises will help, preventing the need for chair backs.

As mentioned there are lots of fancy strokes, but if you perfect these three you will be able to take your canoe where it needs to go. Over time you will intuitively develop and use other techniques to fine-tune your paddling skills.

Navigation for canoers depends on the waters being paddled. For example, it is hard to get truly lost on most rivers. Although you may not know exactly where you are on the river at a given moment, hopefully you know what river you are on and your approximate location. However, when canoeing big lakes of the North Country or coastal areas like the Outer Banks, things can get a little more complicated. Why? Because there is simply more water and more directions you can go than on a river. When river canoeing, you basically follow the waterway downstream. Flatwater paddlers can go all over lakes and coastal areas. After factoring in islands, bays, tributaries, tides, campsites, and portage trails, having a navigation plan makes sense.

Even if you are river paddling, but more importantly for flatwater paddling, your tools for navigation are a GPS with map downloading capability, a compass, and maps—topographic, nautical, aerial, or specialty—for the specific locale you are paddling. Topographic maps display the USGS survey quadrangles, showing roads, trails, streams, elevation, and land cover. Nautical maps not only display islands, passes, channels, channel markers, and so on but also reveal water depths, which can help when canoeing through tidal waters. Aerial maps are photographic satellite imagery. I don't like using aerial maps because they typically don't have features named nor do they show elevation, plus the images can be a little fuzzy. However, aerial maps, downloadable over the internet, are increasing in popularity as a substitute for nautical charts and topographic maps. Some areas have specialty maps, such as Minnesota's Boundary Waters Canoe Area Wilderness, which is covered by Fisher Maps.

No matter whether you use topo maps, nautical charts, or an aerial map along with a GPS, you must have a creative mind to look at your surroundings and place the locale on the map. You are going from three-dimensional reality to two-dimensional maps. The map view of a given destination is from the top looking down, from the sky looking down on the water, a vertical vantage. Your real-life view is from the water surface looking across the water, a horizontal outlook. At this point your mind must be able to turn the vertical map view on its side, to a horizontal view. You must match actual features in front of you with the features on the map. This becomes easier over time and is a function of experience with maps.

Most canoers use a GPS of some form these days, whether a dedicated device or a smartphone application. Some navigate with downloaded maps; others just use GPS as reassurance. The variety of models can boggle the mind. I use a

Garmin eTrex with map downloading capability. I simply download the appropriate nautical charts or topos onto the GPS, and it shows where I am overlain on the chart. You can add caches, campsites, hunting and fishing hot spots, and other features to help you navigate. If relying on downloaded maps, just be careful not

Paddler studying a map. *Johnny Molloy*

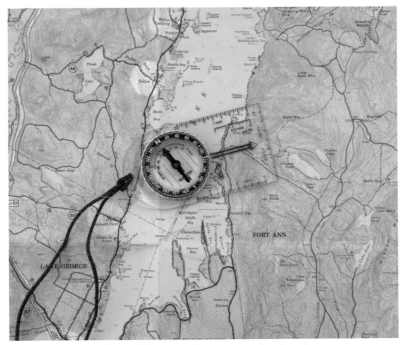

Wise paddlers are well versed in map and compass use. *Stephen Gorman*

to stare down at the GPS all day I have seen unnamed paddling buddies do this, exploring the virtual canoeing world rather than the real waterscape in front of them.

GPS devices can be constantly helpful on the water (there are waterproof marine models out there). After hooking the GPS lanyard to something in the canoe, I turn mine on and just let it go. I can check miles traveled, average speed, average moving speed, amount of time stopped, time of day, sunrise and sunset, and more, all while tracking my current location.

Bring extra batteries, and consider housing your GPS in a waterproof storage case if it isn't waterproof. Canoers who rely only on a GPS are fools, since batteries can die, and I have seen salt water kill a GPS. Breakage and loss can happen too. Finally, remember that the local conditions in front of you trump whatever the GPS says. Some people will not believe they're where they are simply because the GPS tells them otherwise.

Map and compass is the time-honored means of navigation. Wise paddlers should learn and stay well versed in map and compass use. When choosing a compass, you can get as fancy as you want, but a simple one with a clear plastic base, movable compass ring, cardinal points, and numerical degree calibrations will do. To find which direction to go, point the direction-of-travel arrow on the plastic base toward your destination on your nautical chart. Turn the compass housing ring until north on the housing ring lines up with the north of the actual compass arrow. Line up the map north with the compass north.

Depending on where you are, you may or may not have to factor in magnetic declination. Magnetic declination, also known as magnetic variation, is the differential between magnetic north and true north. Magnetic declination changes over time. Before embarking on your trip, you can find the declination from a handy little website at www.magnetic-declination.com. Simply enter your location, get the declination, set the difference between true north and magnetic north, and away you go.

Remember, while perusing a map at home, it is a simple matter to run your finger over the paper, making your way through Florida's Ten Thousand Islands, circling Alaska's Savonski Loop, paddling the St. Regis Canoe Area in New York's Adirondacks, and so on. It is another matter in the field, although the slow pace of a canoer can be an advantage, as the setting changes slowly. Conversely, the slow pace makes mistakes less forgivable.

If you are inexperienced with map and compass, practice by paddling some simple, less-confusing flatwater destinations, then work your way up to more complicated waterways. A GPS with downloadable maps will raise your level of confidence, no matter your skill level.

Other Navigational Considerations

When flatwater paddling, especially in populated coastal areas, motorboats can be your navigational ally. Say you are crossing Blackwater Sound in the Florida Keys, trying to reach The Boggies, a channel leading into Florida Bay from Blackwater Sound. A motorboat is on the same route. The west end of Blackwater Sound looks like one continuous shore from your vantage. You can watch the motorboat power to the unseen channel, helping you figure out exactly where The Boggies are. Also, don't be afraid to flag down a boater and ask for directions (though it can be as embarrassing as pulling into a gas station in a strange city and asking for directions, especially if you are a man).

Birds can be your navigational allies as well. Say you are paddling a shallow bay. The tide is going out and the water is becoming very shallow ahead. Yet from where you are the water seems to stretch across the bay. But then you see birds standing in the water ahead. You know to avoid those shallows. Same goes for

Distance and horizon can make the landscape look different from reality. *Johnny Molloy*

shallows in rivers—if a heron is standing with the water barely above its feet, don't paddle that way.

Distance and horizon can make the landscape look different from reality. When paddling huge lakes and coastal zones, distant islands you are paddling for may not be visible on the horizon. Get your position, set your direction, and trust your compass or GPS. Similarly, far-off features, such as a tributary feeding a huge lake, may be indistinguishable in the distance, but will become clearer as you approach them. Again, set your direction and trust your compass or GPS.

Numbered channel markers are very helpful for navigation. The Coast Guard maintains large red-and-green numbered signs designed for boat navigation along large rivers, harbors, and passes along the US coast. They are normally marked on nautical charts and thus can reveal an exact spot, apprising you of your location.

Other canoeing destinations may have specific markers for that place. Everglades National Park's Wilderness Waterway is marked for approximately 100 miles, from Flamingo to Everglades City. Canoe trails in Georgia's Okefenokee Swamp are signed as well. In other places portage trails or campsites may be marked, giving you exact positions with which to work.

Portage trails or campsites may be marked, giving you exact positions with which to work. *Johnny Molloy*

The Wilderness Waterway, at Everglades National Park, is marked with these signs. *Johnny Molloy*

Obviously the sun can also be used throughout the day to help you figure out your position. Keep up with where you are at all times using all these navigational helpers. Don't paddle for an hour and only reposition yourself every now and then. The more you stay on top of your position, the less likely you will get lost. Finally, do not, I repeat, do not, enter backcountry flatwater canoeing destinations without the proper map and compass, even if you have a GPS.

Night Paddling

Canoeing at night is a viable option in flatwater destinations. It is especially enjoyable on a full moon night, and is a good way to use the tides if in salt water or to avoid windy days anytime. Don't expect to find your way around narrow creeks and small tidal inlets or through a plethora of islands, but less complex areas, like along an unbroken lakeshore or coast, can be paddled when the sun is down. It can also extend your travel capabilities, such as when you're late getting to your destination. GPS devices have a "night mode" that can be reassuring to night paddlers. After you get going, turn off your headlamp or other light source and let your eyes adjust to the darkness. After a while you will be comfortable paddling by moon- and starlight. It can be a beautiful—and smart—experience.

Canoeing at night is a viable option in flatwater destinations. *Johnny Molloy*

LOADING AND UNLOADING YOUR CANOE

Proper—and improper—loading of your canoe affects the floating and paddling performance of your boat. An important rule for loading a canoe is to distribute the weight evenly, front to back and side to side. Too much weight in the front may cause the boat to dig and possibly fill with water when going through a rapid or into waves. Too much weight in the back may cause the boat to drag through shallows and steer poorly. A high bow will also catch the wind.

I often see solo paddlers in the back of a two-seat canoe with nothing in the front to counter their weight. The tip of the canoe is pointed skyward, leaving little surface contact between the boat and the water, making it difficult to steer and subject to wind. This problem is simply corrected. Weigh down the front of the canoe as close to the tip of the bow as you can. Fill a cooler with water, close it, and place it as far forward as possible. You can also use water jugs or other containers. An anchor works as well. If nothing else is available, use rocks. This added weight, known as ballast, will not only keep the boat level but also add stability. Solo paddlers can also turn the canoe "backward" and use the bow seat to paddle from, which will move their position forward in the canoe. If canoe camping, a solo paddler can simply put all gear in the front of the watercraft.

I often see solo paddlers in the back of a two-seat canoe with nothing in the front to counter their weight. *Stephen Gorman*

An important rule for loading a canoe is to distribute the weight evenly, front to back and side to side. *Stephen Gorman*

Always factor the weight of the paddlers when distributing gear in the canoe. *Stephen Gorman*

Uneven side-to-side weight distribution is a major cause of tumping, or tipping, as an uneven canoe can list at precisely the wrong time. Do not underestimate the importance of proper side-to-side weight distribution. While paddling, the unbalanced canoe will lean to the heavy side, making sitting in the boat uncomfortable and switching sides with your paddle more difficult. The longer your paddle day, the more you'll notice this.

Always factor the weight of the paddlers when distributing your gear in the canoe. If you can't weight the boat evenly, then weigh down the rear more than the front. It's better to drag than to dig.

Canoers must consider not only gear weight but also placement of gear. For travel efficiency, keep your gear as low in the boat as possible, preferably below the gunwales. Paddlers on a day canoe trip shouldn't have a problem with this, but canoe campers sometimes carry big loads. Think about wind. A lower profile means less wind resistance for your loaded boat. A higher profile not only catches more wind, but items above the gunwales also have a greater chance of leaving the boat in a mishap, or simply in a gust of wind.

Create space for items you may want close at hand—smartphone, a personal dry bag with sunscreen, cooler, lunch, beverages, binoculars, or a fishing rod. Before departing on a major canoe trip, do a dry-run packing of your boat so you

Hitch your personal dry bag to your thwarts or seat, so if you take a spill your gear won't float off in the current. *David Ramsay*

A properly loaded canoe will help you better negotiate moving water. *David Ramsay*

can get an idea where to place your gear and, more importantly, not have too much gear once at the launch.

Store valuables such as keys and wallet in a dry bag—and strap that bag to the canoe! I once lost a dry bag with my keys and wallet in the midst of a whitewater run on the Smokies' Abrams Creek and didn't notice until we reached the take-out. It was a long and rough walk back up the stream (in it, through it, and around it) before I gratefully found the bag innocently swirling in an eddy. Hitch the dry bag around a thwart or strap it in. If you are going through potentially rough water, use straps to connect your gear to the canoe, including big dry bags full of gear. Hitch the gear to your thwarts, so if you take a spill your gear won't float off in the current. Flat straps with simple pull-through hitches are sufficient.

A word about unloading: When pulling up on a beach or shore, waves or moving water can rock the boat after the paddlers have exited. A canoe full of camping gear should be swiftly unloaded after landing, as the canoe may turn sideways with the waves and then swamp. With two paddlers in waves, one person should stay with the canoe, keeping it upright, while the other rapidly unloads. When the canoe is emptied, pull it to shore well above the waterline. In gentler water, secure the boat with ropes or beach on land before you begin unloading.

When planning a canoe trip, your first thoughts are probably paddles, life jackets, and your canoeing destination. However, don't overlook what you will wear while canoeing, for comfortable, smartly clad paddlers just might get that edge needed to make the most of their canoeing experience.

Starting at the top, consider your canoeing hat. I prefer wide-brimmed, light-colored sun hats to keep Sol at bay. Summer models have built-in ventilation, while

Starting at the top, consider your canoeing hat. I prefer wide-brimmed, light-colored sun hats, to keep Sol at bay. *Johnny Molloy*

thicker ones will have a stiffer brim that is better for windy conditions. Still others drape cloth down around your neck, "French Foreign Legion" style, for added sun protection. For cooler, rainy conditions, use a Gore-Tex-lined hat—it'll keep your noggin warm and dry. All hats should have a drawstring cord to cinch the hat onto your head for windy conditions, and also to flip the hat onto your back when not in use. Avoid ball caps—they allow too much sun on your head, and a wind gust will send them into the water. You can purchase hat clips that latch your cap to your shirt. Your neck deserves attention too. This is where an all-purpose bandanna comes in. I use an oversized one and tie it around my neck for added sun protection.

Next, consider your shirt. You want protection from sun, bugs, and the elements in general, and a shirt that is loose enough for paddling freedom of movement. In cooler conditions, consider layering a collarless T-shirt and a long-sleeve button-up collared shirt. When canoeing through a spring day, temperatures rise and fall. You need to be prepared for temperature variations. A button-up shirt offers more temperature adjustments than does a pullover shirt. Another good choice is the "flats shirt," originally designed for waters of the Florida Keys. These shirts are lightweight and have added ventilation. I prefer shirts with pockets, to store small

In cool to cold times, canoers need additional clothing.

items such as a whistle or lip balm. Muted colors and patterns that blend in with the surrounding scenery are preferable for all canoeing clothes. Hooded sun shirts are increasing in popularity and often protect the hands. They come in a variety of thicknesses and fabrics; some can protect against bugs as well.

On cool to cold days, canoers need additional clothing. Factor in freedom of movement when layering. Fleece or down jackets are a great third layer over a T-shirt and long-sleeve shirt. I recommend zip-up jackets, as they are easier than a pullover to put on and take off in a canoe. They also allow the most comfort variation—simply adjust the zipper to meet your needs. If you are trying to save weight or you anticipate less cold conditions, consider taking a down vest or jacket. Vests allow even more arm movement while canoeing.

Precipitation happens while canoeing. One early June in Minnesota's Boundary Waters, I faced cool, windy, and drizzly conditions. I had just received an Arc'teryx rain jacket and pants to test out. By the end of the trip I was sold on the jacket and pants, as they kept me warm and dry. If you are going to invest your precious time in canoeing adventures, then invest in a good rain jacket. The quality of rain jackets has improved immensely over the past few decades. I remember (and not fondly) the days I wore a cheap clear snap-up jacket while floating down the river, or a bright yellow slicker. Today, primarily due to the improvements of waterproof, breathable fabrics such as those created by Gore-Tex, canoers can stay dry, comfortable, and protected from the wind. However, be prepared to pay for this quality. You will thank yourself when in the middle of nowhere getting bombarded by precipitation, yet staying amazingly dry. Look for Velcro cuff tighteners on your jacket—paddlers raise their arms while stroking, and a loose cuff allows moisture in.

If you are going to invest your precious time in canoeing adventures, then invest in a good rain jacket. *Johnny Molloy*

Cold-weather canoeing can be brutal on hands. Neoprene gloves or even mittens keep hands dry. Alternatively, cheaper wool or synthetic options can be covered by a durable rubber glove.

On cold days, driving rain and chilly winds blowing over open water can be brutal. By all means, bring rain pants when canoeing. I try to have a pair with me at the ready when rain is imminent. They will also protect from the wind while on open water, as will your jacket. Ponchos are unsuitable. They do little for wind protection, do not cover your legs, and are clumsy for a paddler.

For canoers, thin yet tightly woven pants are the best. Ideal are pants that protect you from the sun and bugs, yet dry out quickly. Go with synthetics and avoid cotton. The array of modern materials allows for comfortable-on-the-skin yet quick-drying fabrics. I'll often wear long pants even on warm summer days simply because they provide the best protection from the sun.

Convertible pants are also popular. These function as both long pants and short pants since they have a zipper around each leg in the thigh area to zip off the lower two-thirds of the pants. Convertible pants save weight and space. However, always bring a second pair of pants when canoeing, in case you go for an unexpected swim in the pants you are wearing.

Socks keep your feet warm and also keep underwater debris—especially sand—from entering your shoes if you are on gravelly rivers or beach locales. When canoeing, socks will often get wet, when stepping into the water or from splashing or while loading the boat. You'll want to have an extra pair, and keep them dry. Today's wool socks have a blend of other fibers that keep them itch-free, pliant, and durable.

I mostly count on getting my feet wet while canoeing, whether in the boat or entering and exiting. Weather permitting I wear sandals sans socks. Be discerning when purchasing canoeing sandals. Use sandals with a sturdy sole and straps that wrap over your foot and around your heel. This keeps them on should you take an unexpected dip or simply step out of the canoe in fast-moving water. Do not use slip-on sandals or cheap rubber flip-flops. I use sandals from the Chaco company—they are sturdy, ergonomically sound, and stay on your feet whether you are swimming through a rapid, looking for wood at a riverside campsite, or taking a side hike from the

Sandals with sturdy soles and straps that wrap over your foot and around your heel are best for canoeing. *Stephen Gorman*

81

lake. However, when on a dedicated whitewater run, closed-toe shoes are the best option.

Expedition environments, especially remote ones with portaging, demand closed-toe footwear as well. Options range from old tennis shoes to expensive canoe-specific footwear. If you plan on getting your feet wet but still want a full shoe, consider Merrell's Moab Ventilator. The Moab offers foot support but is designed to drain water from the boot. This way your entire foot is covered, yet the boot is water-friendly. It comes in low-top or high-top models.

Temperature dictates your footwear inside a canoe. Rubber boots are the ticket if temps are cold and you want to keep your feet dry. They make it easier to get in and out of the boat since you can step into the water without getting your feet wet. Obviously you can't step in water above your boot tops, but many rubber boots extend well up to your knee. Neoprene socks will help keep your feet warm inside cold rubber boots.

Avoid going with bare feet in a canoe. You may have to step onto a rocky shore or jump from the boat in an emergency. A friend of mine went without shoes or socks for several days on a blistering hot summer canoe trip on Florida's Ochlocknee River. His feet became extremely sunburned and swelled painfully. Don't go barefoot. Instead, make a good choice of canoeing shoes to meet your needs.

Thinking about your canoeing attire isn't as exciting as floating a wild river or paddling a scenic lake, but a well-clad paddler can stay focused on the scenery instead of trying to stay comfortable.

12 TRAVELING WITH YOUR CANOE

Sound judgment when loading and traveling with your canoe lets you focus on the river trip rather than the drive to the venue. Canoes are generally carried atop a vehicle en route to the water. How you load your canoe depends on what type of vehicle it is and also whether you have an aftermarket roof rack. No matter how you carry your boat, tie it down securely, for the sake of not only your canoe but also your fellow drivers who can be endangered if your boat comes loose.

Some vehicles come factory equipped with roof racks—some sturdy and others less so. Test your rack on a short trip first. Be prepared for wind noise when driving at highway speeds. A friend once loaded his brand-new canoe on his car and sped off to meet me, but then turned around, thinking the wind noise generated by the canoe was an engine problem!

I once saw a canoe—one I had borrowed—fly off the car I was following. Luckily it landed in the median of a busy four-lane highway. On another occasion I saw what a boat can do to a car after sliding over the side of the car while still tied on in the front and rear (it tore the passenger side doors up!). After cinching your boat down, drive a short distance, then pull over and recheck your tie job. I recommend using flat straps with buckles versus ropes for attaching the canoe to the car racks—they stay cinched down better. Simple cinch straps are less complicated than ratchet straps. And purchase top quality tie-down straps; they are what holds the boat to your vehicle.

How to Secure Your Canoe

Putting your canoe atop your car for transport is also known as car topping. Strapping the boat down in four places is a safe and smart idea. Cinch your canoe to the roof racks with straps and then tie it down with ropes from the bow and stern, following these steps and tips.

Carefully lift the boat up and over the car, upside down and parallel with the vehicle, then slide it onto the two crossbars of the roof rack. Throw a strap over the canoe and pull it under the first rack. Keep the straps flat with the boat and not twisted, which can loosen the tie job and also make incredible vibrating noises when your vehicle is moving. Next, flip the strap back over the top of the canoe, then run it back under the rack on the other side of the car. Finally, run the strap through its buckle and cinch it down. Repeat the process with the other rack. Now you have the body of the canoe strapped down in two places, east and west on

83

Strap your canoe down to the racks themselves with straps. *Stephen Gorman*

the car. If your canoe sticks out excessively from the back of the vehicle, tie a red bandanna or piece of cloth to the boat end to signal other motorists. (In some states it is the law.)

Next, secure the front and rear of the canoe, north and south. First, tie the canoe's stern line to the vehicle's rear tow hook (if it has one) or other spot on the frame, not the body. When tying low on the car, make sure to not leave any loose line that could get caught in the wheels or axles. Lastly, tie the bow line to the front underbelly of the car frame. This is especially important since a rogue canoe will fly up in the front first. Whether using straps or ropes, when you are tying onto the front of your car, make sure to put something between the strap and the car body so as not to rub the paint off your vehicle.

A quality aftermarket roof rack installed atop your vehicle is the safest way to transport boats. Invest in one of these if you canoe frequently. Roof racks can be customized to different types and numbers of boats as well. Consider locks for your racks too. Roof racks aren't cheap and can be simply unhitched from your car if not locked down.

Foam Blocks

Foam blocks are used on cars without roof racks, and are squared-off hard foam pieces with grooves, bought at canoe retailers. You slide the four blocks on the canoe gunwales, spread about 4 to 6 feet apart, depending on the size of the car roof, then set the canoe onto the car upside down. Throw the first tie-down strap over the front-center of the boat. Open the car door on the far side, then run the strap through the car and back out the other side door. Cinch down the strap. Do the same thing for a second strap over the rear-center of the boat. Proceed with the bow and stern lines as described above.

Canoe Trailers

Some canoers use trailers to transport their boats. This is most often done when moving multiple canoes, but single-model trailers are available and are smaller versions of your typical boat trailer. Other models carry four to six boats and even up to ten at a time, and are usually used by outfitters or groups. Canoe dollies are two-wheeled contraptions that hitch under or to one end of the canoe, allowing you to roll it from your car to the put-in. These can help a single canoer tote their boat, especially if the carry to the put-in is a long distance, and as long as the terrain isn't rougher than what a four-wheel-drive car can handle.

Other Canoe-Carrying Tips

- If going on a long trip to the put-in or carrying lots of gear, load your vehicle and check your engine *before* you load the canoe. A loaded boat and cinched bow and stern straps prevent rear car hatches and hoods from being fully opened without loosening the straps.

- Many car garages are low and won't allow a car with a loaded canoe adequate overhead clearance. Don't drive into your garage with the canoe still atop your vehicle!

- Check and replace sun-weakened or frayed straps, as a boat is only as secure as its weakest strap. Secure excess loose ends of straps atop the canoe, lest they flap the car to death and drive you crazy.

- Watch for strong winds that may slide your boat atop the racks, loosening the straps. Consider adding L-shaped brackets (highly recommended) to

Canoes properly loaded on vehicles can lead to paddling adventures like this. *Johnny Molloy*

your rack to prevent the canoe from sliding side to side. If sliding occurs, pull over, readjust your canoe, and re-cinch the straps.

- If bothered by wind noise, consider adding a fairing to the front bar of your rack. These angled panels, extending between the car and rack, push wind over the rack and reduce whistling.

- A canoe adds drag and cuts down on gas mileage. Driving at a slower speed while carrying a canoe will help with gas mileage.

- Finally, be careful when walking around a car topped with a canoe. I have seen many a person bump their head on the canoe end sticking out from the car.

River canoe trips require a shuttle. Setting up these shuttles can be a pain, but the payoff is getting to continually canoe new waters in an ever-changing outdoor panorama. The closer you are to home, the more likely you are to be self-shuttling. When making a shuttle for the first time, do as much map work on the front end as possible. Many shuttles in backcountry areas require trips over dirt or gravel roads, bouncing you and your canoe around. A wrong turn or getting stuck in the mud can eat up precious river time.

Look for shuttle directions in outdoor guidebooks or on the internet. Try to find safe take-out landings, such as those at state parks. Always remember to go to the take-out point first, leaving a car there, with the put-in point car following. When at a landing, look around and gauge it for safety, especially scouring the ground for broken car glass. Go with your gut instinct. I have had my vehicle broken into at an iffy put-in. Do not leave valuables in your car! Take your keys with you (*especially the keys for the shuttle car downriver*) and store them securely while you are

Use outfitters for local knowledge and forgoing taking two cars to your river of choice. *Johnny Molloy*

An outfitter on a quiet lake. *Johnny Molloy*

floating. Consider finding a nearby homeowner or business and paying them to let you park. A few bucks can be worth the peace of mind.

Outfitters can save you the hassle of finding the put-in and take-out points on a river and also allow you to leave your car in a safe, secure setting. Outfitters are knowledgeable about the river you plan to canoe and can help tailor a trip to suit your sightseeing, angling, and camping desires. Of course, you will pay for this service.

I frequently use outfitters, not only for their local knowledge and to eliminate the car safety issue but also to forgo having to drive two cars all the way to a chosen river. This especially helps on river trips that are far away from home. Everyone can pile in one car, saving gas and money. Finding canoe outfitters can be as simple as an internet search. Once you have found a few operators for your desired river, call each of them. Often, they operate different stretches of the river or only offer shorter shuttles.

Make sure the outfitter will provide a shuttle the length you desire. Don't be afraid to ask about prices, distances, reservations, and riverside camping, along with everything from rapids to fishing conditions to shoreline landownership to potential weekend crowds. Be very discerning with the information you receive, keeping in mind that outfitters obviously want you on their river.

Outfitter competence can vary. Once, while on the Piney River in Middle Tennessee, the outfitter got her car stuck delivering us to the put-in, delaying our trip by hours. My brother was madder than a hornet! But I have had other outfitters who were very perceptive and set me up ideally.

Outfitters operate on remote rivers as well as suburban streams. Have realistic expectations for each. When on a busy river near a major metro area, such as the Little Miami River near Cincinnati, be prepared to be herded like cattle into vans and debark at peopled put-ins. On the other hand, in more remote areas you have greater personal interaction with the outfitters and may glean a few nuggets about your upcoming aquatic adventure while on the shuttle ride.

Outfitters also operate in wilderness flatwater destinations, including distant and remote places such as northern Ontario. Floatplane shuttles are common in Alaska. Less exotic flatwater outfitters run on small lakes in county parks as well. The first time I went to Minnesota's Boundary Waters Canoe Area Wilderness, I lodged with an outfitter and received a one-on-one routing session as well as a shuttle to our lake entry point. It was expensive, but the competent outfitter set us

A ride on a floatplane can enhance your canoeing experience. *Johnny Molloy*

up on a grand trip. I have since been back to Minnesota's lakes over fifteen times. Consider using services such as this when going for the first time to an unfamiliar canoe wilderness. Remember, it's all about getting on the water. Being shuttle wise and outfitter savvy can enhance your canoeing experience.

If you paddle a canoe long enough, you are eventually going to portage. Portaging is the act of carrying your canoe from point A to point B on land in the midst of a paddle, most often from lake to lake in the wilderness, or around a particularly tough rapid in a river. You may also find yourself portaging around an unforeseen obstacle in a river or waterway, such as a huge fallen tree.

Portaging is a part of many fine canoeing destinations, from portage-heavy places such as St. Regis Canoe Area in New York, to places where portages are occasional such as Maine's Allagash Waterway, to places with single portages such as Big Shoals on Florida's Suwanee River or Angel Falls on the Big South Fork National River in Tennessee.

Portaging involves not only transporting your canoe but your gear as well. Most portages have been used as portages for as long as people have been traveling down those waterways; therefore your typical portage trail is well established. Portages are measured in rods. A rod is 16.5 feet, the length of an average canoe; 320 rods equals a mile.

Portaging is a part of many fine canoeing destinations. *Johnny Molloy*

Before trying to carry the canoe and all your gear with you at the same time, start with simply carrying the canoe. You will use this technique not only for portaging between bodies of water but also for simply getting the canoe from car to lake or river. One of the most difficult parts of a portage is getting the canoe over your head and onto your shoulders in order to carry it. For the one-person "flip" first, tip the canoe onto its side with the bottom facing you. Bend down, place your knees under the canoe, and grab the thwart, then raise the boat to your lap. Now, grab the far side of the gunwale with the arm closest to the bow, and in one motion flip the canoe over your head and rest the middle thwart or yoke onto your shoulders. Steady the boat with your arms in front of you and begin walking forward, keeping the front of the canoe higher than the rear, allowing you to see ahead. This flip can also be done with two or three people, accommodating smaller paddlers or really heavy boats. Usually the other two people are to the bow and stern of the middle person, who will be carrying the canoe.

Alternatively, consider the two-person lift: Persons A and B stand at the front of an overturned canoe, one on each side, and lift that end. After the front is lifted, person A bridges the canoe from under the front half of the boat while B walks under the lifted canoe and settles their shoulders onto the center thwart, then stands up to begin carrying the canoe.

Portage wheels are used to transport canoes at some destinations. *Johnny Molloy*

First, tip the canoe onto its side with the bottom facing you. Bend down and place your knees under the canoe.

Lean over the canoe and grab the far thwart with your left hand.

Pull the boat up so the side perches on your legs.

In one motion raise the canoe over your head.

Rest the middle thwart or yoke onto your shoulders, facing toward the front of the canoe.

Steady the boat with your arms and begin walking forward, keeping the front of the canoe higher than the rear, allowing you to see ahead.

Some portages close to put-ins can be busy. Avoid lollygagging, and don't eat lunch or fish from these portages. Sometimes, especially earlier in spring, portage trails can be muddy. Try not to swing around the muddy parts of the trail—it only widens the mudhole. Also, if the bugs are biting, wear long pants and a long-sleeve shirt. Have the bug dope and head net ready. Carrying a canoe on top of your head and steadying it with both hands makes you a great mosquito target!

At some destinations, such as British Columbia's Bowron Lakes Provincial Park, portage wheels can be used to transport your canoe and gear. Two wheels linked by an axle beneath a "cradle" on which to set the canoe are used to roll the canoe—and some gear inside the boat—from one lake to the next. A paddler is stationed at each end of the canoe to guide and propel the boat forward on the

The 17-foot Wenonah Spirit II is ideal for portaging and paddling, too. *Johnny Molloy*

trail. These portage wheels ease the burden but must be carried in the canoe while tripping.

In some places, such as Minnesota's Boundary Waters Canoe Area Wilderness, portage wheels are expressly forbidden. Check ahead before attempting to use portage wheels.

Some he-men try to carry not only the canoe but also their gear all at once over a portage. The water may be calling, but who's in that big of a hurry? Besides, I don't feel like getting a hernia out in the backcountry. I suggest one person carry the canoe, and the second person carry the biggest piece of gear. Leave the rest behind where you landed. On short portages, carry the canoe or gear all the way to the other end, where you will once again jump in the canoe. Go back to the landing and retrieve the rest of your gear. Do a double-check so as not to leave anything behind.

On longer portages it's better to do what is known as staging. Carry the canoe as far as you can. When you begin to tire, look for two closely spaced trees between which you can lean the front tip of the canoe, so the boat won't have to be lifted again to resume portaging. Then go back and retrieve what gear is left and carry it to the canoe or beyond. Next, backtrack to the canoe and carry the boat forward. The other person is doing this as well with the gear. Be wary about leaving a food-filled pack unattended if you have seen bear evidence in the vicinity. Staging allows you to rest and alternate between walking and carrying the canoe or gear.

With two canoers in one boat, determine the first portage by flipping a coin; whoever loses does the first portage, then the second person does the next portage and so forth. This way whoever gets the hard portages is left to the luck of the draw. It'll pretty much even out over the long haul.

If you plan on portaging regularly, it is wise to use gear designed for ease of portaging. The most important item is a lightweight canoe constructed with portaging in mind. Canoes such as those built by Wenonah are designed to be carried from lake to lake via portages. I highly recommend the 17-foot Wenonah Spirit II. At 42 pounds this ultralight Kevlar boat can perform in the water and not break your back on a portage. Portage yokes make life easier too. These are shoulder pads that you can mount to the thwart of a canoe. These aftermarket items aid greatly not only in comfort while portaging but also balance. Large dry bags with shoulder straps, or time-honored Duluth packs, allow you to concentrate your gear and carry it efficiently across portage trails. With the right gear and good strategies, portaging can be a pleasant connector between canoeing waters.

Canoe camping is a great way to enhance your paddling experience and spend more time in the watery wilderness that we like to explore. Canoe camping separates you from the crowds, from those paddlers literally unwilling to take the extra time and preparation to load their gear and take it to their favorite stream or lake. Canoe campers paddle with the satisfaction that they don't have to turn around before dark, knowing that they will enjoy overnighting on the shoreline, with the enticing waters reflecting the starlight above.

And when you arise in the morning, more canoeing pleasure lies ahead. Canoe camping makes the most of your drive and shuttle times, because once you make the drive to the put-in you get to enjoy more bonus hours on the water than is possible on a simple day trip. For many of us, the lure of canoeing is not always the water, but the places through which the water flows. Canoeing is just the excuse—and the means—to head into the back of beyond, to enjoy nature on nature's terms, to get past the parking lot to a world apart from our daily lives.

Canoe camping is a great way to enhance your paddling experience. *Johnny Molloy*

The joy is found in paddling an Appalachian trout stream bordered with rising green mountains, or a winding mangrove maze in the Everglades; casting for bass along a sun-splashed Ozark river where inviting gravel bars offer campsites below magnificent bluffs; or enjoying the reflection of a North Woods lake on a sunny summer day. That is canoe camping.

When you embark on your trip, you need not worry about returning to the put-in that day, since you will be camping out. Your overarching consideration becomes distance traveled per day and finding campsites each evening, all adding up to ending at your chosen endpoint—or returning to your starting point—at the prescribed time.

When canoe camping you are not only paddling yourself and the normal gear you would carry on a day trip but also camping gear and food. The simple weight of the extra gear slows you down and requires more effort to move the canoe. Knock off 0.5 mile per hour while canoe camping versus day tripping on a given type of water. Other than the extra weight of the canoe, many other considerations are the same. River trippers will have current on their side, lake canoers will negotiate winds, and coastal canoe campers will consider tides and more. Add time for loading and unloading your canoe, especially at the beginning of a trip. It may take two or three attempts to properly load your gear.

I try to average between 8 and 15 miles per day while canoe camping. Before your trip starts, come up with an overall plan. Say you have a 60-mile river trip over six days. Your goal is to try to average 10 miles per day. Look at a map and find markers to make each day—side streams, landings, campsites, bridges. This will help keep you on track.

Consider time spent paddling relative to whatever else you want to do. The faster and harder you paddle—or the shorter each travel day—the more you can engage in non-paddling pursuits. Sometimes, however, water conditions keep you in the canoe longer than planned. For example, when the winds are blowing, canoers may be forced to paddle harder and longer just to keep on course. Stream paddlers may have slower currents than anticipated. Waves can be high along the coast. This all eats into your time at camp spent photographing, fishing, or whatever you like to do. Find a balance between time in the canoe and time at camp, while adapting to the daily conditions on the water.

No matter what happens, be prepared to roll with the punches. I have spent canoe camping trips completely stranded by post-rain high waters on a river and high winds on lakes and coastal waters. Storms come up, canoers get tired, a campsite is so desirable you want to spend more time there, canoes need repairing, someone gets sick, and more. Conversely, I have been pushed downriver by strong

Find a balance between time in the canoe and time at camp. *Johnny Molloy*

currents, moved faster than planned by eager paddlers, and blown across lakes by favorable winds. When distance-altering situations arise, adjust your distance goals and daily time spent in the canoe.

Finding Waterside Campsites

Four of us were canoeing the Jacks River in Missouri. It was our last night of a five-night trip. The temperatures were in the mid-70s, and we were enjoying the Ozark waterway and the scenery on all sides. That evening, as the sun sank below the horizon, we came upon a curve in the river. A spectacular bluff rose across the Jacks, overlooking a huge gravel bar with plenty of level spots. High water had left copious driftwood to burn for warmth in the cool evening. We gently landed the canoes. My brother Mike proclaimed it the perfect campsite, and it was.

Despite this ideal story, finding a perfect canoe campsite at the right moment can be as rare as an eclipse. Locating a campsite from water is not always as easy as it sounds. When floating on water you are at the lowest point around and always looking up at the land, which makes it challenging to discern level tent spots and kitchen and bathroom sites.

In some places, such as Kentucky's Cumberland River, you must get out of your boat and physically look for a suitable campsite. Be prepared to seek campsites along sloped and/or wooded shores, where you must climb to a good camp. After

Lake campsites can be found near tributaries, on larger islands, inside bays, or on points like this one. *Johnny Molloy*

you travel many rivers for many years, patterns where campsites are located will become clear. Camping flats can be at the confluence of two streams. Camping sandbars and gravel bars can often be found on the inside of sharp river bends. Therefore, perusing a map for sharp river bends or the confluence of streams can yield potential campsites. Depending on the terrain, potential lake campsites can have patterns too. Look where tributaries feed the lake, on larger islands, on points, and inside bays.

When looking for a boat landing, seek a moderate slope to land your canoe. It doesn't have to be perfect, just good enough to hold your boat. Gravel bars and beaches make great landings. Also look for the mouth of a tributary flowing into the waterway on which you are floating. The tributary mouth forms a break in the shoreline, allowing you to land your boat and access a campsite. Make sure to secure your boat once at the campsite, then pull out anything you want to stay dry and not lose (see sidebar).

Sandbars look like great campsites from the water, and they can be. They are unencumbered by vegetation, can be easily leveled without damaging the environment, and generally have fewer insects. The downside is the sand itself. It can—and will—get in your sleeping bag, in your tent, in your food, and just about everywhere else. And when it rains, sand sticks to everything.

I prefer gravel bars to sandbars. Depending on the size of the gravel, the bars can have the positive traits of a sandbar without all the particles of sand getting on everything. Gravel bars do not provide as good a sleeping environment as do sandbars, but you can find places that can be leveled out and made into superlative sleeping spots. Look at the downstream end of a gravel bar, as it will have the smallest granules and hence the best spots to pitch your tent. Gravel bars also sometimes have trees growing from them to provide shade. Before you camp on a gravel bar, think about how these bars were formed—from high-water flooding. If heavy rain is likely and there is a chance of flooding, do not camp on a gravel bar or sandbar. Seek dry land above visible high-water marks.

Campsites don't always appear at the precise moment you want to set up camp. Allow yourself ample time to find a spot, especially if there are other canoe campers nearby. Start with expecting Shangri La, then temper your desires. Prepare to lower your expectations as the day gets late. Pick a campsite and stick with it. Sometimes a bad campsite starts looking better after you've settled in.

Certain canoe camping destinations have designated backcountry paddler campsites, such as Everglades National Park or Georgia's Okefenokee Swamp. These sites must be reserved in advance, and you must stay at your chosen campsite on the given day specified in your camping permit. You should stick to your itinerary

A pleasant campsite on a giant sandbar on the Mississippi River. *Johnny Molloy*

Certain canoe camping destinations have designated backcountry paddler campsites, such as Everglades National Park. *Johnny Molloy*

if possible. Other places, like Boundary Waters Canoe Area Wilderness, have designated backcountry campsites (around 2,000 of them!), but they are first-come, first-served, no reservations. You are also not allowed to camp at a spot that is not designated for camping. Be sure to use the designated sites, preserving the resource, unless emergency conditions dictate otherwise.

Leaving a Canoe Improperly Secured at Camp Can Have Bad Consequences

It had been a hot, sunny day of canoeing on Mississippi's Black Creek. We headed onto a gravel bar a little early, casually threw up camp, and relaxed in the shade of a sycamore tree. That evening thunder rolled and lightning crackled upriver. Ours was gratefully a rainless night.

Next morning I awoke to fog and stumbled down to the river for coffee water. My canoe was gone! Overnight the river had risen enough to float the boat away, despite no rain falling on us. Our paddles, life vests, and other assorted gear were in the canoe too. Disaster! Surely if we were lucky enough to find the canoe, it would be overturned and minus our gear. Luckily, there were four of us and we had two boats.

My brother Mike and I sped downriver in the remaining canoe, sans coffee but fueled by adrenaline, looking for the runaway boat. We went over one shoal, then another. No boat. Because of the fog we were worried we would miss the boat entirely, though the river was narrow. But then, ahead, a green shape appeared—the canoe! It was lodged into a low-hanging tree, facing perfectly downstream as if it had been guided by paddlers instead of the whim of the current. Amazingly, our paddles, fishing equipment, and gear were intact. Only my pride was compromised.

Always pull your boat well above the body of water on which you are paddling, especially rivers, and especially when thunderstorms are likely. It can rain upstream of your camp but not rain on you, just like in my misadventure, then the river will rise and take your boat away. If I expect a potentially ultrahigh rise, I'll pull the canoe way up and tie it onto a tree or my tent pole for good measure.

Lost campsite canoes are not limited to rivers. When rain falls, a canoe partly pulled onto a lakeshore can float away. The lake rises a bit from the rain, and the boat fills with rainwater, which helps it slide into the water. Add a little wind and presto—no more canoe. Also, if rain is predicted, don't leave your gear in the boat, because when the canoe fills with rainwater, items inside can become inundated.

Wind alone can make canoes magically disappear—if you haven't pulled your boat ashore securely. While on West Virginia's Greenbrier River, my pal Kent Roller and I were eating lunch on a big rock right by the canoe, then spotted a grazing deer. We left our spot to check out the critter—and returned to see the boat floating away before our eyes. Kent bravely dashed through the water for our canoe. He slipped on some algae and went headfirst into the water, smashing his shin on a rock and getting a nasty cut. We should've pulled the canoe up farther.

Whether you are leaving your canoe for a brief pit stop, lunch break, or overnight camp, always take the extra moment to secure it in some way. Then you won't be faced with troubles on the water that could have been easily prevented. For longer stops consider pulling the boat entirely out of the water and turning it over, then storing the contents under the canoe to keep them dry and secure.

Always pull your boat above the body of water on which you paddle.

If you paddle enough (a good thing), at some point you will need to repair your canoe. The most common problems that arise are seat deterioration and wearing through layers of the canoe bottom from abrasion or an unexpected gash from hitting a rock.

Canoe seat repairs are generally simple, and are done at home, not in the field. Paddlers normally "ride out" partially torn seat webbing until returning home, since an uncomfortable seat doesn't affect the performance and seaworthiness of the canoe. Repairing a canoe seat is a simple matter of taking out the old seat, frame and all, then replacing it with a new seat, rather than reweaving the cane or webbing around the old seat. Seat kits are found at outdoor shops and on the internet. Go with a replacement from the manufacturer of your canoe if possible. Also, go ahead and replace both seats, because if one seat is rotted, the other is not far behind. Simply remove the old seat and screw the new one into the seat mounts. A non-brand-specific seat may need a little hand sawing to fit. To ensure a good fit, when you remove the old seat, place it atop the new one then cut the ends to match, as well as the screw holes. You are ready to go! Whether your seat is new or old, check the seat-mount bolts to make sure they are tightly screwed into the canoe itself.

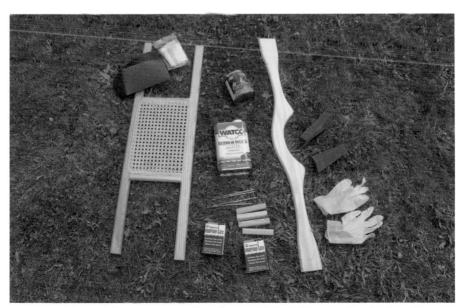

Both canoe seats and thwarts can easily be replaced with the right accessories. *Stephen Gorman*

A roll of duct tape can sometimes be your best friend. *Stephen Gorman*

Problems with the canoe body, such as punctures or deep abrasions, can be more complicated. Yes, it is true that duct tape can be a canoer's best friend on the water, used to temporarily close leaks and staunch the flow of water from gashes or to cover worn thin spots. It is the most practical short-term solution. When using duct tape, dry the area to be taped as much as possible, and tape both the inside and outside of the canoe. Hopefully you can make it to your take-out for long-term repairs. A word of caution: Despite the value of duct tape in quick fixes, it leaves the area to be repaired covered in sticky adhesive, which needs to be removed before repairing the boat for good.

Canoe patch kits generally consist of a fiberglass cloth patch, along with resin, a brush, and plastic gloves. Before repairing anything, first prepare the surface to be patched. Remove any debris and loose pieces of boat, and start with a dry surface. Resin comes in two containers, and mixing the two creates the bonding liquid. Be ready, as the resin hardens quickly. Mix the resin and smooth it onto the canoe with a brush, then apply the patch. Saturate the patch with resin and let it harden.

Paddlers can preemptively add skid plates to high-abrasion areas on their canoe. *Johnny Molloy*

Patch the inside and outside of the canoe if possible, though it may take two separate steps. After the resin is fully dried, sand the patch smooth and paint if desired.

Canoers can preemptively add skid plates to the bottom of their boat, most often at each end. These are precut fiberglass cloth patches that are affixed onto the canoe at high-abrasion areas. I recommend skid plates—they extend the life of a canoe.

Today's canoes are made of numerous materials and composites. Patch kits are specifically made for different composites, so make sure your patch kit is compatible with your canoe. The best way is to check with the manufacturer.

APPENDIX A: CANOEING CHECKLIST

- ☐ Bailer
- ☐ Boat sponge
- ☐ Canoe
- ☐ Car keys for vehicle at end of river run (if paddling end to end)
- ☐ Dry bags for gear storage
- ☐ Duct tape
- ☐ Maps in map case, or GPS with downloaded maps
- ☐ NOAA weather radio
- ☐ Paddles
- ☐ Personal flotation device (PFD)
- ☐ Spare paddle
- ☐ Sunglasses, sunscreen, lip balm
- ☐ Towline
- ☐ Whistle

Other items you may want to consider depend on your personal interests as a paddler: fishing gear, smartphone in dry case, trash bag, camera, watch, extra batteries—especially for your GPS—binoculars, and wildlife identification books.

Johnny Molloy

APPENDIX B: CANOE TERMINOLOGY

Bailer
A cup or other device used to scoop water from the bottom of the canoe

Bottom curve
Curve of the canoe bottom from one side of the boat to the other

Bow
Front area of the canoe; refers to an area, rather than a specific part of the canoe

Deck
Small covered part on each end of the canoe, level with the gunwales

Depth
Area from the top of the gunwales to the bottom of the canoe

Draft
Depth of the boat under the waterline

Dry bags
Waterproof bags, primarily made of rubber and/or plastic, with a watertight seal

Flare
Outward curve of the sides of the boat

Flatwater
Still water without current; a lake, pond, or portion of ocean without tidal current

Foot brace
Metal rod or wooden plank along bottom of canoe to stabilize a canoer's feet

Freeboard
Height of boat above the waterline

Gunwales
Also spelled *gunnels*; the upper rails of the canoe. The gunwales run atop each side of the canoe from tip to tip, bow to stern

Keel
Nautical term for the centerpiece underlying a boat from bow to stern, to which the frame of a boat is attached. For canoes, the keel is the ridge running along the bottom of a canoe from front end to back end

Knee pads
Foam glued to the bottom of the canoe for comfort as you paddle with your knees down on the canoe bottom

Painters
Ropes tied onto each end of the canoe

PFD
Personal flotation device, more commonly known as a life vest

Port
Side of the canoe to your left

Portage yokes Shoulder pads that you can mount to the center thwart of the canoe to make portaging more comfortable

Portaging The act of carrying your canoe from point A to point B on land in the midst of a paddle, most often from lake to lake in the wilderness, or around a particularly tough rapid in a river

Rocker Curve of the keel line between bow and stern

Saddle Seat used by whitewater paddlers when placing their knees on the bottom of the boat with their feet pointed back

Skid plate Precut fiberglass cloth patches that are affixed onto the canoe at high-abrasion areas

Splash cover A waterproof cover fitted over the canoe with snaps and used to prevent rapids and waves from splashing over the gunwales into the canoe, also known as a spray deck

Staging Carrying your canoe and gear in stages over a portage, rather than carrying it all from end to end of the portage

Starboard Side of the canoe to your right

Stern Back of the canoe; refers to an area, as does the bow, rather than a specific part of the canoe

Thwart A crossbeam linking the sides of the canoe at the gunwales, or upper rails of the canoe. Thwarts support and stabilize the canoe, and preserve the integrity of the canoe's shape

Tumblehome Inward slope of the upper side of the canoe, from the middle of the canoe sides up to the gunwales

Whitewater Fast-moving water in rapids, often foaming as it dashes over rocks and other obstacles

Yoke A curved "neck ring" in the center thwart of the canoe, used for portaging your boat

INDEX

Index

ABOUT THE AUTHOR

Johnny Molloy is a writer and adventurer based in Johnson City, Tennessee. His outdoor passion started on a backpacking trip in Great Smoky Mountains National Park while attending the University of Tennessee. That first foray unleashed a love of the outdoors that has led Molloy to spend most of his time hiking, backpacking, canoe camping, and tent camping for the past three decades. Friends enjoyed his outdoor adventure stories; one even suggested he write a book. He pursued his friend's idea and soon parlayed his love of the outdoors into an occupation. His efforts have resulted in more than eighty-five books—so far. His writings include guidebooks on camping and paddling, comprehensive guidebooks about specific areas, and true outdoor adventure books covering the eastern United States. Molloy has also authored these FalconGuides, among others:

Best Easy Day Hikes Cincinnati
Best Easy Day Hikes Greensboro and Winston-Salem
Best Easy Day Hikes Jacksonville, Florida
Best Easy Day Hikes Madison
Best Easy Day Hikes New River Gorge
Best Easy Day Hikes Richmond, Virginia
Best Easy Day Hikes Springfield, Illinois
Best Easy Day Hikes Tallahassee
Best Easy Day Hikes Tampa Bay
Best Hikes Near Cincinnati
Best Hikes Near Columbus
Best Hikes Near Asheville
Coastal Trails of the Carolinas
Exploring Mammoth Cave National Park
Hiking Waterfalls Tennessee
Hiking Waterfalls Pennsylvania
Hiking Waterfalls Kentucky
Hiking Waterfalls West Virginia
Hiking New Jersey
Hiking the Berkshires
Hiking Kentucky
Paddling Georgia
Paddling Tennessee
Paddling Virginia and West Virginia

Molloy also writes for various magazines and websites. He continues to write and travel extensively throughout the United States, participating in a variety of outdoor pursuits. His non-outdoor interests include American history and University of Tennessee sports. For the latest on Molloy, please visit johnnymolloy.com.